Business and **Human Rights**

in a time of change

Christopher L. Avery

About the report

Amnesty International UK Business Group

The Amnesty International UK Business Group, established in 1991, exists for the purpose of encouraging companies:

- to be aware of the human rights impact of all aspects of their operations;
- to use their legitimate influence in support of human rights in all countries in which they operate;
- to give effect to the Universal Declaration of Human Rights;
- to implement Amnesty International's Human Rights Guidelines for Companies;
- to include a specific commitment to human rights in their statements of business principles and codes of conduct;
- to make their human rights policies explicit, ensuring that these are integrated across all function, monitored and audited.

The author

Christopher Avery is an international lawyer, with degrees from Stanford University, University of California (Davis) School of Law and Columbia University School of Law. He was Legal Adviser and a senior manager at the International Secretariat of Amnesty International from 1983 to 1993. More recently, he advised transnational companies on the development of human rights policies. Currently he is developing social benchmarks for corporations in the developing world, based on field research he conducted in South Africa and Asia. He has had articles published in Stanford Journal of International Law, Interights Bulletin, and two books: Liability of Multinational Corporations under International Law *(Kluwer International Law)* and Democracy, Human Rights and the Rule of Law: Essays in Honour of Nani Palkhivala *(Butterworths)*.

This report first appeared in November 1999 on the author's website, "Business and Human Rights: reports by Christopher Avery/Links to other websites" <http://www.business-humanrights.org>

Purpose

This report is intended to further discussion on business and human rights and to provide senior managers with terms of reference and sources of information to assist them in the development of company policy.

Amnesty International UK
99-119 Rosebery Avenue
London EC1R 4RE
Tel: +44 (0)20 7814 6200
Fax: +44 (0)20 7833 1510
http: //www.amnesty.org.uk/business

February 2000

Contents

Foreword

The purpose of *"Business and Human Rights in a time of change"* is to provide terms of reference and sources of material for company managers responsible for policy development in this area. This is not a statement of Amnesty International's policy, but an assiduously researched survey of the field

The author, Christopher Avery, provides a comprehensive and scholarly tour d'horizon illustrating the context and the drivers of change which are propelling companies towards new norms of policy with regard to the protection of human rights. The many elements in the transformation of business thinking covered in this paper include the growth in ethical investment, developments in social auditing methodologies, shareholder resolutions, selective purchasing laws in the United States, dialogue with NGOs and the movement towards the incorporation of universal human rights standards into the economic bloodstream.

The parameters of the emerging debate are set out within a coherent structure, supported by extensive references. There is a clear message here for all transnational corporations – *human rights is rapidly establishing itself as a key component of the debate on corporate responsibility. As the forces of globalisation continue to gain momentum, society increasingly demands that transnational corporations improve their performance in the area of human rights. Failure to address these demands will prove damaging to a company's most important long-term asset – its reputation. Silence and inaction no longer constitute a defensible response.*

Sir Geoffrey Chandler
Chair Amnesty International UK Business Group

Further guidance for companies, illustrated with extensive case studies, are provided in a primer, "Human Rights – are they any of your business?", published jointly by Amnesty International UK and the Prince of Wales Business Leaders Forum.

Looked at:

Companies:

■ Nike ■ Enron ■ Unocal ■ Shell ■ BP ■ Reebok ■ Body Shop ■ Levis ■ Tata

People:

■ Aung San Suu Kyi ■ Desmond Tutu ■ Amartya Sen ■ Peter Drucker

Countries:

■ Myanmar (Burma) ■ China ■ India ■ Nigeria ■ Philippines ■ South Africa ■ Vietnam

Topics:

■ Human rights and business ■ Human rights and development ■ Codes of conduct ■ Independent monitoring ■ Sweatshops ■ Changes in business thinking ■ Effect on business performance ■ Consumers ■ Employees ■ Reputation ■ Shareholder resolutions ■ Socially-responsible investment ■ Universal Declaration of Human Rights ■ United Nations ■ ILO ■ European Parliament ■ Amnesty International ■ Human Rights Watch ■ Oxfam

See the Table of Contents and Index for a complete list of subjects

Overview

This report surveys recent initiatives by companies, human rights advocates, governments, the United Nations and others. It identifies sources of pressure on business to act responsibly, how this pressure is intensifying, and how business is responding. It shows how quickly events are moving, and how important it is for companies and for human rights advocates not to be left behind.

Until the mid-1990s, relatively little attention was paid to the activities of business with regard to human rights. This changed in 1995, when Ken Saro-Wiwa and eight others were executed in Nigeria. They had campaigned against environmental damage by oil companies, including Shell. They were tried by a special court that clearly violated international fair trial standards. Shell refused to criticise the trial. One Shell manager said: 'I am afraid I cannot comment on the issue of the Ogoni 9, the tribunal and the hanging… Nigeria makes its rules and it is not for private companies like us to comment on such processes.' Intense international criticism of Shell's human rights record followed. The company has since announced new human rights policies and practices 'to ensure we act in the best possible way when confronted with human rights issues.'

Since 1995 many other companies have found their human rights record under the spotlight; most of them were unprepared (see the case example of Nike, in Section 5 of this report). As 'globalisation' (and concern about some of its social effects) accelerates, it is clear that the labour and human rights practices of multinational corporations will be even more closely scrutinised in the decades ahead.

Some companies have taken initiatives to demonstrate that they accept the principle of accountability for their human rights record. Many have adopted codes of conduct referring to human rights issues. In 1995-96 The Body Shop commissioned an independent audit of its social performance and published the results. Other companies are beginning to allow some degree of outside monitoring; many more will do so in the coming years in response to a range of pressures - reputational, regulatory, competitive, media, consumer, government, shareholder, stakeholder.

Until the mid-1990s the private sector seldom appeared on the radar screen of human rights and development organisations. Now many of these groups engage with business, promote standards of corporate conduct, monitor company practices, and campaign against abuses. Each year they give increasing priority to their work with business.

United Nations Secretary-General Kofi Annan has announced a Global Compact for business. UN High Commissioner for Human Rights Mary Robinson speaks regularly about business and human rights. One UN body is drafting a human rights code of conduct for transnational corporations.

Companies still tend to be stronger on rhetoric than action when it comes to human rights. However, smart companies are beginning to recognise that the move towards accountability for human rights is strong and unstoppable. Those companies that fail to move from rhetoric to meaningful action will suffer damage to their reputation and financial bottom line, sooner or later.

Introduction

What is the nature of the radical transformation that is changing the relationship between society and business? ■ What are the characteristics of a successful company in this new environment? ■ What is meant by human rights?

Peter Drucker, a leading authority on international business and management, in 1993 wrote a best-seller called *Post-Capitalist Society*.[1] That book says we are now living through a sharp transformation that comes along every few hundred years. The transformation this time is a shift to a knowledge society. In capitalist society the means of production were capital, land and labour. Now in post-capitalist society value is created by knowledge, productivity and innovation. Now employees rather than capitalists own both the 'means of production' (their pension funds are the largest shareholders of most big companies) and the 'tools of production' ('knowledge workers own their knowledge and can take it with them wherever they go').[2]

Lester Thurow, a professor of economics and former dean of the Sloan School of Management at MIT (the Massachusetts Institute of Technology), agrees with Drucker, referring to 'a technological shift to an era dominated by man-made brainpower industries'[3]:

Consider this list of the twelve largest companies in America on January 1, 1900: the American Cotton Oil Company, American Steel, American Sugar Refining Company, Continental Tobacco, Federal Steel, General Electric, National Lead, Pacific Mail, People's Gas, Tennessee Coal and Iron, U.S. Leather, and U.S. Rubber. Ten of the twelve companies were natural resource companies. The economy at the turn of the century was a natural resource economy....[O]nly one of these companies, General Electric, is alive today....

In contrast, consider the list made in 1990 by the Ministry of International Trade and Industry in Japan speculating as to what would be the most rapidly growing industries in the 1990s and the early part of the twenty-first century: microelectronics, biotechnology, the new material science industries, telecommunications, civilian aircraft manufacturing, machine tools and robots, and computers (hardware and software). All of them are man-made brainpower industries that could be located anywhere on the face of the earth.[4]

Drucker notes that this transformation to a knowledge society is a time of great flux, raising basic questions about society and its values. As multinational corporations expand their operations worldwide, many observers are raising questions and concerns about globalisation and its effects.[5] Jeffrey Garten, Dean of Yale University's School of Management, wrote in *Business Week*: 'In the twilight of the 20th century, making globalization work humanely is quickly becoming the dominant issue of our time.'[6]

The business community's relation to human rights is coming under the spotlight, and the questioning of values is well underway. This report looks at some of the changes taking place in that domain, and their implications. It is important for companies – and for human rights advocates dealing with companies – to recognise these fundamental changes and to adapt to the new world.

Smart companies are already adapting to the new culture of human rights accountability.

Drucker says that in the new knowledge society, the successful companies will be those organised for constant change and innovation, always ready to change products, procedures and policies: 'It must be organized for systematic abandonment of the established, the customary, the familiar, the comfortable.'[7] He says the successful companies will be those that focus on responsibility rather than power, on long-term success and reputation rather than short-term gain.[8]

But too many companies still resist calls on them to give serious attention to human rights issues, thereby putting their reputation and bottom line at risk.

Chapters 1 and 2 identify trends that have a bearing on business and human rights. *Chapters 3 and 4* look at how companies are responding to those trends. *Chapter 5* summarises the case history of Nike and its Asian factories: how one company resisted and responded to society's demand that companies get serious about human rights. Nike's human rights record continues to be watched closely. *Chapter 6* presents some observations drawn from discussions with multinational companies about human rights issues. *Chapter 7* discusses company-supported projects in the developing world aimed at promoting sustainable development and human rights.

While this report covers only some of the recent developments and initiatives relating to business and human rights, the footnotes refer to publications that provide a fuller picture.

The term 'human rights' is used in this report to refer to the full range of rights in the United Nations (U.N.) Universal Declaration of Human Rights[9]: civil and political rights, as well as economic, social and cultural rights. These rights are recognised as being universal, indivisible, interdependent and interrelated.[10]

The term 'sustainable development' is used to mean an approach to development that 'meets the needs of the present without compromising the ability of future generations to meet their own needs.' That definition was used in the seminal 1987 report *Our Common Future*, written by the U.N.-appointed World Commission on Environment and Development, which was chaired by Norwegian Prime Minister Gro Harlem Brundtland. [11]

1. Changes in business thinking

What responsibility does business have to society? ■ Is human rights a factor in a company's reputation? ■ How does a company's approach to human rights affect its financial bottom line? ■ Do employees care about the human rights record of their company?

1.1 Re-examining the fundamental purposes of business

In 1970 Milton Friedman wrote that 'the one and only social responsibility of business' is to increase its profits.[12] While there are still remnants of that thinking around, a growing number of business leaders see the equation as more complex: they consider that making money for shareholders is necessary, but not sufficient. For example:

i) **Jack Welch, Chairman and Chief Executive Officer (CEO), General Electric Company:** 'I've always believed that the greatest contribution a business could make to society was its own success, which is a fountainhead of jobs, taxes, and spending in the community. I still believe that – but I don't think that is enough anymore. And I don't believe that even generous financial philanthropy on top of that prosperity is enough. …[T]hese times…will not allow companies to remain aloof and prosperous while the surrounding communities decline and decay.'[13]

ii) **Ratan Tata, Chairman, Tata Industries:** 'We would like to make sure that community development is…treated as something as important as any other operation of the Tata group.'[14]

iii) **the late JRD Tata, Chairman of Tata Sons from 1938 to 1991:** 'We in the Tatas, have long recognised that the responsibilities and obligations of our industrial enterprise transcend the normal ones to its owners, its employees, and to the customers of its products and services, and that they should encompass the welfare of, and service to, the local community and society as a whole….'[15]

iv) **Michael R. Bonsignore, CEO, Honeywell:** 'As we move into the twenty-first century, it is increasingly clear that the key elements of social responsibility – especially how we support our workers, their lives, and communities – will be key elements in a company's productivity and competitiveness.'[16]

v) **Kenneth Mason, President, Quaker Oats:** 'Making a profit is no more the purpose of a corporation than getting enough to eat is the purpose of life. Getting enough to eat is a *requirement* of life; life's purpose, one would hope, is somewhat broader and more challenging. Likewise with business and profit….[We should] encourage, not evade, discussion of those problems that arise when the activities of business conflict with the needs and concerns of society.'[17]

vi) **Gerald M. Levin, chairman and CEO, Time Warner Inc:** 'Our position as the world's leading media and entertainment company could not have been reached – and could not have been sustained – solely from business success. It rests equally on our tradition of social responsibility and community involvement. At the core of this enterprise is the determination to make a difference as well as a profit.'[18]

vii) **Sir John Browne, Group Chief Executive, BP Amoco:** 'We're part of society and we have some responsibility to contribute to its positive development. That covers issues such as human rights and employment and, for my industry in particular, the question of global warming.'[19]

viii) **George Soros, President of Soros Fund Management, Chief Investment Advisor to Quantum Fund, Founder of Open Society Institute:** 'The doctrine of laissez-faire capitalism holds that the common good is best served by the uninhibited pursuit of self-interest. Unless it is tempered by the recognition of a common interest…, [our democratic open society] is liable to break down.'[20]

The 'Tomorrow's Company' Inquiry, headed by Sir Anthony Cleaver (then Chairman of IBM U.K.), made the following observation in its 1995 report: 'The companies which will sustain competitive success in the future are those which focus less exclusively on financial measures of success – and instead include all their stakeholder relationships, and a broader range of measurements, in the way they think and talk about their purpose and performance.'[21] Sir Anthony Cleaver remarked about the report: 'We have tackled the sterile debate over shareholder versus stakeholder head on. We believe that only by giving due weight to the interests of all key stakeholders can shareholders' continuing value be assured.'[22] The 'Tomorrow's Company' Inquiry, which brought together senior executives from 25 of the top businesses in the United Kingdom (U.K.), had the following aim: 'to stimulate greater competitive performance by encouraging UK business leaders and those who influence their decision-making to re-examine the sources of sustainable business success.'[23] The inquiry's report includes this conclusion:

Tomorrow's Company recognises its interdependence with the community in which it operates. It develops leadership strategies which strengthen both the climate for business success and the community itself.

Yesterday's Companies stick to an insular view. They see the communities in which they operate as either a neutral factor in their success or a potential source of interference to be resisted.[24]

The inquiry also reached the following conclusion relating to business and the environment (which today also applies to business and human rights):

Tomorrow's Company recognises the critical importance of achieving environmental sustainability in the interests of all stakeholders and accepts the challenge this poses.

Yesterday's Companies view environmental concerns as peripheral and react defensively when issues arise.[25]

Mark Goyder, director of the London-based Centre for Tomorrow's Company (an independent organisation which grew out of the 'Tomorrow's Company' inquiry), remarked recently: 'The old idea – which is still prevalent on Wall Street – is that companies which talk a lot about stakeholders and accountability are actually betraying their shareholders. I'd say that's a 20th century view of the 21st century problem.'[26] He says that to succeed in the next century companies need to build long-term trust with shareholders and stakeholders by reporting on their progress on human rights issues.[27]

Columbia University's Graduate School of Business now offers a seminar on 'Transnational Business Practices and International Human Rights.'[28] Harvard Business School and INSEAD have introductory courses on the purpose of business, including coverage of social issues such as human rights.[29] The Asian Institute of Management (Manila), selected by *Asian Business* magazine as one of the five best business schools worldwide, has made 'development management' one of its full-fledged business degrees.[30] Its Center for Development Management trains students to combine hard-nosed management skills with a commitment to addressing issues such as sustainable development, poverty alleviation, health, education and the environment.[31]

Royal Dutch/Shell, in its recently-revised Statement of General Business Principles, says Shell companies recognise five areas of responsibility 'seen as inseparable': to shareholders; to customers; to employees; to those with whom they do business; and to society.[32] Shell's 1999 social report says:

We must take economic, environmental and social considerations into account in everything we do. We will embrace the concept of sustainable development in our business decisions, large and small. In this way we will continue to create value for our shareholders and society, while being responsive to society's changing expectations. We will evaluate the economic, environmental and social impact of our options and strive to get the balance right in our decisions. This will mean that some business decisions will be made differently and some may have different outcomes from the past.[33]

Shell's social report goes on to say:

Why bother producing a report on our contribution to sustainable development when the Group is under such harsh financial pressure? Should we not put all our efforts and resources into ensuring a profitable future? This, we believe, is exactly what we are doing. Our values, Business Principles, commitment to contribute to a sustainable form of development – and the candid reporting of our performance in those areas – are inextricably linked to our long-term commercial success. Sustainable development builds the platform on which business thrives and society prospers.[34]

It is becoming mainstream to talk about the responsibilities companies have to stakeholders and communities. In March 1999 *Business Week* magazine announced a forthcoming special advertising section entitled 'The Next Bottom Line: Agenda for the 21st Century':

Solving social and environmental challenges is no longer optional for companies or society. These global challenges demand ingenuity and resolute efforts to sustain economic progress while preserving the vitality of our communities and the integrity of the Earth's natural systems. Business Week and World Resources Institute (WRI) are proud to announce a definitive special advertising section, The Next Bottom Line. The section will feature essays by CEOs of major corporations and insightful articles by WRI addressing how business can balance new social, environmental, and financial expectations and still provide shareholder/stakeholder value.[35]

The *Business Week* special advertising section, which appeared in May 1999, included contributions about social and environmental issues by the CEOs of AT&T, BP Amoco (on 31 December 1998 BP and Amoco merged), Intel, General Motors, DuPont, Storebrand ASA, Mitsubishi Electric, Weyerhauser, ITT Fluid Technology, and Siemens Westinghouse Power. C. Michael Armstrong, Chairman and CEO of AT&T, wrote: 'AT&T understands the need for a global alliance of business, society and the environment. In the 21st century, the world won't tolerate businesses that don't take that partnership seriously, but it will eventually reward companies that do.'[36]

In the *Business Week* special section's introduction, Jonathan Lash (President, World Resources Institute) wrote:

The social challenge reflects the fact that as the private sector has grown in power and importance, so have the expectations of a diverse group of stakeholders. Stockholders, customers, employees, local communities, and the variety of interest groups that comprise civil society may all have different priorities. With increased visibility for corporate behavior and increased vulnerability for companies that run afoul of today's volatile public opinion, no company can afford to neglect its relationships with its stakeholders or escape the need to be part of building a better society....

These are daunting challenges. But those companies that can simultaneously manage and anticipate new technologies, environmental uncertainties, and stakeholder expectations – that make these challenges central to their corporate strategy – will gain a powerful advantage in the new century. And the social and environmental payoff from companies that manage to this new set of criteria, the Next Bottom Line, could be huge.[37]

The fact that the *Business Week* initiative took the form of an advertising section begs the question: Is there a real change of thinking in the corporate world that affects day-to-day decision-making, or is it more of a public relations exercise aimed at creating the perception of a more socially-engaged private sector? The answer is probably a mix of the two, with some companies giving higher priority than others to implementing real change in their operations.

In any event, more and more company executives are going on the record with a commitment to address social issues, and their company's social performance can now be measured against that commitment as well as against other standards.

Companies – both those which have made a public commitment to social responsibility and those which have not yet done so – need to be asked hard questions, for example:

a) Are you operating in countries or in 'export processing zones' where the internationally-recognised rights of workers are not being respected in an effort to maintain a compliant and inexpensive workforce? What action are you taking?

b) Are you certain that the supplies you buy in China are not being produced by forced prison labour?

c) How are you using your influence to promote human rights?

d) Are you engaged in partnerships with local human rights and development organisations to promote the rule of law and sustainable development?

Too often companies presume that their shareholders have no interest other than short-term profit. Most shareholders are long-term investors who want to invest in responsible companies with the sort of reputation that helps to ensure a sustained record of success. Dayton Hudson, a large, successful retail company in the United States (U.S.), for decades has been one of the most generous companies in the country in terms of its philanthropy. For 53 years Dayton Hudson's commitment has been to donate 5% of its pre-tax profits to community programmes (thereby giving $57 million in 1998, over $1 million per week), including to 'social action programs that assist people in reaching economic independence.'[38] Few if any large companies in the U.S. donate a higher percentage. In 1982-83 Dayton Hudson commissioned a survey of its stockholders to see how they felt about the company's very high level of community giving. Of the 561 shareholders surveyed, 31% supported increasing the level of giving, 42% supported continuing at the same level, and 5% supported a cutback.[39]

John Elkington, Chairman of SustainAbility (a London-based consultancy) and author of *The Green Consumer Guide* and *The Green Capitalists*, urges companies to integrate into their thinking a 'triple bottom line' to which they are already being held to account: economic prosperity, environmental quality, and social justice. He notes:

[W]e are seeing a profound values shift in countries around the world....And a key dimension of this shift is the way in which what would once have been seen as 'soft' values (such as concern for future generations) are now coming in alongside – and sometimes overriding – traditional 'hard' values (such as the paramount importance of the financial bottom line).[40]

Peter Drucker says the private sector greed we saw in the 1980s where 'maximise shareholder value' was the mantra will not work anymore. His view is that just focusing on this year's bottom line forces a corporation to be managed for the shortest term, which leads to a decline in the long-term wealth-producing capacity of business. 'Long-term results cannot be achieved by piling short-term results on short-term results.'[41] Drucker recognises that economic performance is the first responsibility of business, but he says it is not the only responsibility. 'Power must always be balanced by responsibility; otherwise it becomes tyranny. Without responsibility, power...always degenerates into non-performance.'[42] Drucker concludes that political and social theory since Plato and Aristotle focused on power, but in post-capitalist society the focus will be on responsibility.[43]

1.2 Challenging traditional business thinking about human rights

Much of the business community has traditionally argued that human rights do not need to be a priority for developing countries (and that companies operating or investing in countries with repressive governments should not be challenged). The substantive merits of this argument are showing strain. For example:

(a) **Many in the business sector traditionally argued that it is acceptable for governments of developing countries to give a low**

priority to civil and political rights while focusing on economic development. Their theory: respect for civil and political rights will naturally follow later, after trade and investment create a middle class and induce political liberalisation.

That argument ignores the internationally-recognised principle that economic rights and civil/political rights are universal, interdependent and indivisible. It ignores the fact that the U.N. Declaration on the Right to Development affirms: 'All human rights and fundamental freedoms are indivisible and interdependent; equal attention and urgent consideration should be given to the implementation, promotion and protection of civil, political, economic, social and cultural rights.'[44] It ignores The Vienna Declaration, adopted by consensus by the 171 governments at the 1993 U.N. World Conference on Human Rights, which states: 'While development facilitates the enjoyment of all human rights, the lack of development may not be invoked to justify the abridgement of internationally recognized human rights.'[45] Nevertheless in the past business people regularly made that traditional argument (often in relation to Asia), and authoritarian governments welcomed the support.

Given recent events in Indonesia and other Asian countries, that argument is heard less often these days. Kim Dae Jung, democratically-elected President of South Korea, certainly sees things differently: 'I think Asia's economic crisis stems mainly from a lack of democracy....If we develop both democracy and a market economy, we can expect successful results in the near future.'[46]

Amartya Sen, recipient of the 1998 Nobel Prize for Economics, professor emeritus at Harvard University, and Master of Trinity College at Cambridge University, wrote in 1999:

Some ask: 'Is freedom of political participation and dissent conducive to development?' This way of posing the question is seriously misleading. It misses the important point that the substantive freedoms of political participation and dissent are among the constituent components of development. Their relevance to development does not have to be freshly established through their indirect contribution to the GNP or to

the promotion of industrialization; they are part and parcel of what enriches human life.

As it happens, in fact, the often-repeated claim that the denial of political liberty and civil rights helps to stimulate economic growth is not confirmed by the extensive empirical information that is now available on this subject. There is little evidence that authoritarian politics contribute to economic growth, and there are many indications that economic growth is more a matter of a friendly economic climate than a harsh political system. Furthermore, economic development has other dimensions. Economic insecurity can more easily survive under authoritarian governments, which deny democratic rights and do not have to face multiparty elections, uncensored news reporting, or open public criticism. It is thus not surprising that no famine has ever taken place in a functioning democracy (even very poor ones).

In fact, the argument has a much more extensive reach than the connection between democracy and famine prevention. Protection of the destitute created by sudden economic change (caused by financial or other crises) is also far too sluggish when the protective power of democracy has been given little chance to flourish. The East Asian crises provide ample examples of this.

Freedom is not only the primary end of development, it is also one of its principal means. In addition to acknowledging the foundationally evaluative importance of freedom, we also have to understand the empirical connection that links freedoms with each other. Political freedom (in the form of freedom of speech and elections) helps to promote economic security. Social opportunities (such as education and health facilities) contribute to individual freedom and communal prosperity. Economic prospects (like opportunities for participation in trade and production) can help to generate personal abundance as well as public resources for social facilities. All of these freedoms strengthen each other.[47]

A study of 123 countries for the period 1985 to 1994 suggested that there is no meaningful statistical correlation between increases in foreign direct investment and improvements in a country's human rights performance.[48] Another study, by the Organization for

Economic Co-operation and Development (OECD), found no convincing causal connection between trade liberalisation and respect for freedom of association rights.[49] In fact the OECD study found that a country's desire to increase trade and direct foreign investment could lead to a deterioration rather than an improvement in human rights: '[T]here [was] evidence that some governments felt that restricting certain core labour standards would help attract inward FDI [foreign direct investment].'[50] In some countries foreign direct investment has been seen as a factor in reinforcing a government and insulating it from calls for democratisation.[51]

A recent article argued that unless a process of economic liberalisation incorporates human rights considerations from the beginning, it will lead to 'a race to the bottom' and exacerbate human rights abuses:

To the extent that the transnationalization of investment has engendered a global chase for the cheapest labor markets, international investment practices inevitably drive down wage levels as developing countries compete for foreign investment. In this setting, it has become increasingly difficult to persuade governments of developing countries to respect internationally-recognized labor rights, particularly the right to receive a wage that meets the 'basic human needs' of workers…In the longer term, this phenomenon has in many developing countries apparently retarded further expansion of the middle class, and instead has widened the economic gap between laborers and the management class. Against this background, it is increasingly difficult to assume that investment in and of itself will promote expansion of a middle class, thereby enlarging the number of citizens who enjoy economic and social rights and simultaneously making it more likely that citizens will insist upon personal and political freedoms. In this respect too, then, whether foreign investment promotes human rights depends – in this instance, on whether the foreign investor assures adequate conditions of work, including fair wages.[52]

Amnesty International said in a 1996 publication about China: 'The government says the right to subsistence and development is paramount for the Chinese people. But the need to feed the hungry can never justify torture, and there is no evidence that denying people such a fundamental right as freedom of speech improves their economic well-being.'[53]

(b) Another argument often put forward by business is that investment and trade with a repressive government should be encouraged because withdrawal by international business or sanctions hurt the people and deprive the country of the liberalising influence of engagement with the outside world.

While business people and others continue to make this case, their persuasiveness is strained when people with the moral authority of Nobel laureates Archbishop Desmond Tutu and Aung San Suu Kyi argue just the opposite.

Desmond Tutu stated during South Africa's apartheid era:

I have no hope of real change from this government unless they are forced. We face a catastrophe in this land, and only the action of the international community can save us….I call upon the international community to apply punitive sanctions against this government to help us establish a new South Africa – non-racial, democratic, participatory and just. This is a non-violent strategy to help us do so….

You hear so many extraordinary arguments. Sanctions don't work. Sanctions hurt those most of all whom you want to help. That is interesting. I haven't heard similar arguments brought forward in the United States when sanctions are applied at the drop of a hat against Panama, Nicaragua, Libya, Poland. I have to say that I find this new upsurge of altruism from those who suddenly discover they feel sorry for blacks very touching, though it's strange coming from those who have benefited from cheap black labour for many years. Spare us your crocodile tears, for your massive profits have been gained on the basis of black suffering and misery.[54]

Aung San Suu Kyi made the following statements in recent years:

If material betterment…is sought in ways that wound the human spirit, it can in the long run only lead to greater human suffering. The vast possibilities that a market economy can open up to developing countries can be realized only if economic reforms are under-

taken within a framework that recognizes human needs.[55]

There are those who claim that the people of Burma are suffering as a consequence of sanctions, but that is not true. We want investment to be at the right time – when the benefits will go to the people of Burma, not just to a small, select elite connected to the government.[56]

Burton Levin, a former U.S. Ambassador to Burma, agreed with Aung San Suu Kyi's conclusion about sanctions: 'Foreign investment in most countries acts as a catalyst to promote change, but the Burmese regime is so single-minded that whatever [income] they might obtain from foreign sources they pour straight into the army while the rest of the country is collapsing.'[57]

Craig Forcese is a Canadian law professor, an expert on business and human rights, and Project Manager for the Business and Human Rights Project of the Canadian Lawyers Association for International Human Rights. He cites four ways that a company's activities, rather than inducing political liberalisation, 'may bolster the repressive capacity and the staying power of a regime which systematically violates human rights':

■ *The firm can produce products used by the regime that increase its repressive capacity....*

■ *The firm can be a major source of revenue that increases a regime's repressive capacity.....*

■ *The firm provides infrastructure in the form of roads, railways, power stations, oil refineries or the like that increases a regime's repressive capacity....*

■ *The firm in the country may provide international credibility to an otherwise discredited regime....*[58]

The *New York Times* ran a lead editorial on 6 December 1998 entitled 'Corporations and Conscience.' It was written in the wake of revelations that General Motors and Ford apparently had helped the Nazis and even accepted medals from Hitler. The editorial includes the following comments:

In recent years companies like Nike and Unocal have embarrassed themselves with questionable overseas partnerships....[F]or the past decade American companies have cozied up to the junta in Myanmar, Afghanistan's Taliban, Central Asia's dictators, African kleptocrats and Colombia's military. American corporations argue that they can be a positive force in repressive countries. This can be true. They often pay better than local companies, and bad publicity has spurred some corporations to sponsor health clinics and other good works. But these benefits are outweighed by the political support companies lend to bad regimes. Few ever criticize their hosts' politics. Governments take their presence as an American endorsement....Unocal, which is a partner with Myanmar's Government in a gas pipeline project, is being sued in American courts for alleged use of forced labor and forced expulsion of villagers. Last week, Unocal did end its efforts to work with the Taliban on a pipeline through Afghanistan, primarily because oil prices are so low....Companies should use their tremendous power responsibly....Some regimes are so heinous that simply to continue making profits under them is reprehensible. Nazi Germany was surely one. Corporate officials are not only businessmen, they are citizens of the world.[59]

1.3 Corporate reputation: A valuable asset

Charles Fombrun, Professor of Management at the Stern School of Business (New York University), says in his 1996 book *Reputation: Realizing Value from the Corporate Image* that each company's reputation is 'a fragile, intangible asset' that 'complements – and sometimes surpasses – the value of the more tangible material and financial assets that managers routinely worry about.'[60] He notes:

Long ignored, intangible assets are now gaining increased notice. In the last few years, those of us who study corporate strategies have begun to recognize that intangible assets may well provide companies with a more enduring source of competitive advantage than even patents and technologies....In recent years, many prominent companies...found their reputations sullied, and so called attention to the importance of protecting and defending reputational capital....This book shows that better-regarded companies build their reputations by developing practices that integrate eco-

nomic and social considerations into their competitive strategies. They not only do things right – they do the right things. In so doing, they act like good citizens. They initiate policies that reflect their core values; that consider the joint welfare of investors, customers, and employees; that invoke concern for the development of local communities; and that ensure the quality and environmental soundness of their technologies, products, and services.[61]

A recent publication by The Prince of Wales Business Leaders Forum, in collaboration with The World Bank and The United Nations Development Programme, commented on the subject of corporate reputation:

Reputation is built on a complex base of intangible attributes such as reliability, quality, honesty, trust, social and environmental responsibility and credibility – which span the whole spectrum of a company's business and support activities. Despite this, and despite the fact that many managers agree that reputation does have value, most companies still adopt a fragmented and PR-driven approach to reputation management.

There is clear evidence that a good reputation gains a company more customers, better employees, more investors, improved access to credit, and greater credibility with government....The difference between a company with ethical capital and one with an ethical deficit – perceived or real – can even determine their 'licence to operate' in some emerging markets.[62]

Sir Geoffrey Chandler, formerly a senior manager at Royal Dutch/Shell, is now Chairperson of Amnesty International's U.K. Business Group. He emphasises that 'the reputation of companies – crucial to their acceptability and success in a critical world – will be increasingly influenced by their willingness to recognise their role' in respect of human rights.[63] He says companies have a clear choice 'to use what influence they have, or to do nothing....If they speak out they may incur the anger of government. If silent, the certain price is reputation – which is, of course, everything.'[64]

Sir John Browne, Group Chief Executive of BP Amoco, addressed the issue of reputation in terms of 'trust' in his introduction to BP's 1997 Social Report:

For any company, commercial success and a highly competitive financial performance are essential. What we are learning, however, is that enduring success requires something more, and that the ability to make a constructive contribution to society and to bring positive energy to the solution of its problems is the key to the development of genuine trust and to all the opportunities which flow from that trust.[65]

1.4 Human rights are good for business

During the period of military rule in Nigeria, Shell Nigeria's general manager reportedly stated: 'For a commercial company trying to make investments, you need a stable environment. Dictatorships can give you that.'[66] Fortunately such views are heard less often these days from business people, though no doubt they have not disappeared entirely.

Thomas d'Aquino, CEO of Canada's Business Council on National Issues, articulates a different point of view about business and human rights:

Whether at the World Trade Organization, or at the OECD, or at the United Nations, an irrefutable case can be made that a universal acceptance of the rule of law, the outlawing of corrupt practices, respect for workers' rights, high health and safety standards, sensitivity to the environment, support for education and the protection and nurturing of children are not only justifiable against the criteria of morality and justice. The simple truth is that these are good for business and most business people recognize this.[67]

Former Canadian Prime Minister Joe Clark rejects the notion that the defence of human rights will mean losing trade. He notes that many Canadian Ministers and diplomats had raised human rights issues with their trading partners without in any sense jeopardising those relationships. He says Canada's reputation for human rights is actually an asset for business.[68]

Reebok's 'Human Rights Production Standards' say: 'Reebok's experience is that the incorporation of internationally recognized human rights standards into its business practice improves worker morale and results in a higher quality working environment and higher quality products.'[69]

Jaime Augusto Zobel de Ayala II, President of the Ayala Corporation (a large Filipino company involved in businesses including real estate, banking, food, and insurance) and President of the Ayala Foundation, made the following comments in a speech to Asian business people at a 1995 Conference on Corporate Citizenship (Hong Kong):

We all pay for poverty and unemployment and illiteracy. If a large percentage of society falls into a disadvantaged class, investors will find it hard to source skilled and alert workers; manufacturers will have a limited market for their products; criminality will scare away foreign investments, and internal migrants to limited areas of opportunities will strain basic services and lead to urban blight. Under these conditions, no country can move forward economically and sustain development....It therefore makes business sense for corporations to complement the efforts of government in contributing to social development.[70]

UCLA graduate school of business Professor David Lewin[71] and J. M. Sabater (formerly IBM Director of Corporate Community Relations) in 1989 and 1991 conducted in-depth, statistical research surveys of over 150 U.S.-based companies to determine whether there is a verifiable connection between a company's community involvement and its business performance. Details of their study and conclusions are published in an article entitled 'Corporate Philanthropy and Business Performance.'[72] They concluded:

Our findings, both cross-sectional and longitudinal, indicate that there are indeed systematic linkages among community involvement, employee morale, and business performance in business enterprises. To the best of our knowledge, this is the first time that such linkages have been demonstrated empirically. Moreover, the weight of the evidence produced here indicates that community involvement is positively associated with business performance, employee morale is positively associated with business performance, and the interaction of community involvement – external involvement – with employee morale – internal involvement – is even more strongly associated with business performance than is either 'involvement' measure alone.[73]

The Lewin-Sabater study examined in detail the question of whether a company's strong community involvement led to strong business performance, or the other way around. They found that a company's financial success did tend to lead to more community involvement, but they also found that increased community involvement did help to drive a company's business performance.[74]

A study by DePaul University Professor of Accountancy Curtis Verschoor published in 1998, examining the 500 largest U.S. public corporations, found 'a statistically significant linkage' between 'a management commitment to strong controls that emphasize ethical and socially responsible behavior' and 'favorable corporate financial performance.'[75] Those corporations which declared a commitment to ethical behaviour towards their stakeholders or emphasised compliance with their code of conduct were found on average to perform better financially than those corporations which did not.

Harvard Business School Professor Rosabeth Moss Kanter noted in 1999 that the leading companies that are using 'their best people and their core skills' to develop innovative approaches to social needs realise that 'social problems are economic problems, whether it is the need for a trained workforce or the search for new markets in neglected parts of cities':

They have learned that applying their energies to solving the chronic problems of the social sector powerfully stimulates their own business development. Today's better-educated children are tomorrow's knowledge workers. Lower unemployment in the inner city means higher consumption in the inner city.[76]

Sophon Suphaphong, President of Bangchak Petroleum (a leading oil company in Thailand), observed: 'The world's markets just won't buy products that are cheap and good quality if they are manufactured by countries that exploit child labour; that are dictatorial; and that destroy the environment. Eventually, business people will have no choice but to take part in the process of resolving our social problems.'[77]

In a 1998 keynote address to an International Symposium on Human Rights and Business Ethics in Bangkok, business leader Anand Panyarachun (formerly Prime Minister of Thailand, Thailand's Ambassador to the U.N., and Chairman of the Federation of Thai Industries) said:

For some time now, companies have been called on to abide by certain environmental standards. Now their human rights standards are also being called into question....In the West, human rights groups, consumers, investors and labour unions, have through various pressure points been successful in promoting human rights in corporate codes of conduct. And companies have been responding to such pressures....Those companies that get bad press about human rights violations have seen consumers boycott their products. In the long run, the bottom line suffers. I would encourage our NGOs [non-governmental organisations] to mount similar campaigns in the interest of protecting human rights in Thailand.[78]

Marjorie Kelly, editor of *Business Ethics* magazine, observed recently:

We're going through a mind-change. Most of us still carry around the subliminal idea that ruthless behavior beats the competition and good behavior is money out of pocket. But the data shows that the traditional idea is wrong. Social responsibility makes sense in purely capitalistic terms.[79]

Allan Willet, the founding Chairman of the Centre for Tomorrow's Company (described in section 1.1 of this report), made the following comment about a stakeholder/community oriented approach to business: 'Make no mistake, this is all about wealth creation and profit. This is not a trade-off at the expense of shareholder value but a powerful way of making sustainable profits and achieving lasting value for the shareholder.'[80]

David Smith, president of the Council for Ethics in Economics, says that human rights performance has become a differentiating factor among companies. 'If people don't have the confidence [that companies are] going to maintain a good image, then the share values may suffer.'[81]

Kleinwort Benson Investment Management's Paul Sheehan explains why his firm launched an investment fund focused on U.K. companies that take a stringent stakeholder approach to their businesses: 'It makes sense. The companies that have clear values, invest more in training employees and put money back into the communities actually buying their products will have more success over the long term than those still caught up in a bottom-line-only culture.'[82]

Speaking to a November 1998 meeting of the American Petroleum Institute, William Cvengros, CEO of investment management company Pimco Advisors L.P., said that in judging the financial performance of companies 'we don't put extra value on environmental activities or citizenship. But we usually find that those companies that are good corporate citizens and have a sound environmental program are also the best investment value.'[83]

Peter Sutherland, the former Director-General of the World Trade Organization who is now Chairman of Goldman Sachs International and Co-Chairman of BP Amoco, said:

Business finds itself having to deal in a practical way with human rights issues. This is not a matter of choice but a reality in this global environment. And getting it right is not only a matter of ethical behaviour and moral choice. Enlightened business people have realised that good business is good business. Good business is sustainable, is part of global society not at odds with it, and reflects values which are shared across the world.[84]

Sutherland points out that it is in the interest of the business community for companies to not only address human rights issues in their own operations, but also to raise concerns about social issues with governments:

Some in business say 'Why should business stand up and lecture Governments on human rights: Our business is to look after our shareholders.' Well, I don't believe that business should stand up and lecture governments on human rights. But I also believe that it is part of building good sustainable businesses to help establish safe, secure, stable and peaceful societies. Business thrives where society thrives. We don't have to look far for an example of this. Look at the investment confidence in Northern Ireland during the first cease-fire and after that cease-fire broke down. It is appropriate for companies to point out to governments the impact of social or environmental policies on commerce. Just as it is appropriate for companies to point out the impact of fiscal policy on commerce....In practice, this must be managed in different ways in different situations. Sometimes publicly, sometimes quietly.[85]

Sir John Browne, Chief Executive of BP Amoco, when defining the interests of international business, says that one of the conditions for best pursuing business is operating in an open society. He recognises that this runs 'directly contrary, of course, to the common belief that companies find it easier to deal with the apparent stability of repressive regimes than to manage the uncertainties of democracy. In fact, stability built on repression is always false. Sooner or later the waters break the dam.'[86] Chris Gibson-Smith, BP Amoco's Managing Director responsible for its policies, observes: 'As human rights has risen on the corporate agenda, multinational businesses are realising that the successful company of the 21st century will be one that can manage its social and environmental performance as effectively as its business one.'[87]

Business for Social Responsibility, an alliance of U.S.-based corporations described in section 3.1 of this report, includes on its website the following statement about the 'business importance' of human rights (a brief explanation of each point in the list is provided on the website):

As the expectations of companies regarding human rights have increased, so too has awareness of the business value of developing and implementing policies and practices to ensure compliance with human rights. Companies that have adopted corporate codes of conduct or other human rights principles and that have taken effective steps to enforce these policies have reaped the following benefits:

■ *Enhanced Compliance with Local and International Laws...;*

■ *Promoting Rule of Law...;*

■ *Managing the Supply Chain...;*

■ *Protecting Brand Image...;*

■ *Enhancing Risk Management...;*

■ *Avoiding Trade Sanctions...;*

■ *Increasing Worker Productivity and Retention...;*

■ *Addressing Shareholder Concerns...;*

■ *Satisfying Consumer Concerns...;*

■ *Building Community Goodwill...;*

■ *Avoiding Negative Campaigns...; and*

■ *Applying Corporate Values....*[88]

Amnesty International has noted that 'the building blocks of human rights protections – the rule of law, government accountability, independence of the judiciary – are the key elements in creating a stable climate for business, as evidenced by the recent economic crisis in Asia.'[89]

1.5 The employee factor

Companies are increasingly recognising that only if they have a good reputation and social record will they be able to attract and retain the best and brightest employees.

Fortune magazine has noted that the single most reliable predictor of overall excellence in a company is the ability to attract and retain talented employees.[90]

Lester Thurow emphasises that in this new era of knowledge-based business, 'when human capital is the dominant factor of production,'[91] it is absolutely essential that a company be able to recruit and keep smart employees:

The firm's only significant asset goes home every night, is an independent decision maker as to where his skills will be employed, controls the effort that she will or will not put into the firm's activities, and cannot be owned in a world without slavery. When a firm's employees leave, the firm's unique ideas and technologies automatically go with that employee to the new employer. Unless the firm can hold on to its employees, proprietary knowledge effectively ceases to exist.[92]

Peter Drucker notes that managing a business exclusively for shareholders alienates the new class of knowledge workers; they 'will not be motivated to work to make a speculator rich.'[93] He says companies and mission statements 'that express the purpose of the enterprise in financial terms fail inevitably, to create the cohesion, the dedication, the vision of the people who have to do the work so as to realize the enterprise's goal.'[94] He concludes: 'Loyalty' from now on cannot be obtained by the paycheck.'[95]

A 1995 study in the U.S. found that 84% of employees felt that a company's image in the community is important; 54% said it is very important.[96] The Wirthlin Group, which surveyed over 2000 U.S. adults in 1993 about their opinions towards corporations, commented in 1995: 'Employees prefer to work for a company that has a good reputation as a corporate citi-

zen. A positive corporate persona enhances a company's ability to attract top talent and results in more productive, more loyal employees.'[97]

In the 1999 book *When Good Companies Do Bad Things*, the authors examine how allegations of corporate irresponsibility (human rights, environmental, and otherwise) have affected the companies concerned and note: 'Intense reactions by employees to accusations of wrongdoing illustrates the depth of their need to feel in sync morally with their employer and their need to believe that their employer is in sync with society's norms.'[98]

Recently several multinational oil company managers mentioned to the author in informal conversations that many of the most promising university graduate engineers are now asking questions during their job interview about the company's policy on the environment and human rights, questions which did not arise often in the past.

2. Society calls on business to act

What are the sources of pressure on business to take human rights seriously? ■ Do the public and consumers care what companies do about human rights? ■ What are the United Nations and governments calling on companies to do with regard to human rights? ■ What steps are human rights advocates urging companies to take? ■ How do shareholder resolutions and socially responsible investment relate to human rights?

2.1 Silence and inaction: No longer tenable options

Royal Dutch/Shell has come under fire for its environmental and human rights record in Nigeria over the years, both for what it has done and for what it has failed to do.[99] Shell's worldwide reputation is still paying the price. Shell sought to distance itself from events in Nigeria when Ken Saro-Wiwa and his Ogoni colleagues (who had campaigned against environmental damage by oil companies and for increased autonomy for the Ogoni ethnic group) were arrested in 1994, detained illegally for at least eight months, held incommunicado in military custody under harsh conditions, tried in 1995 (before a special court established by the military government) under procedures that clearly violated international fair trial standards, convicted of murder, and executed.[100] Shell says of the case: 'We did not seek to influence his trial, but after the verdict the Chairman of the Group's Committee of Managing Directors sent a letter to the Nigerian head of state urging him to grant clemency for all those sentenced.'[101]

One of Shell's general managers reportedly made the following statement after the execution:

I am afraid I cannot comment on the issue of the Ogoni 9, the tribunal and the hanging. This country has certain rules and regulations on how trials can take place. Those are the rules of Nigeria. Nigeria makes its rules and it is not for private companies like

us [Shell] to comment on such processes in the country.[102]

That statement ignores the most basic concepts of human rights: governments are prohibited from violating internationally-recognised fundamental human rights, and human rights violations are a matter of international concern because human rights transcend national boundaries. While the statement came from Shell, the philosophy of 'human rights is not a matter for business to get involved with' has been shared by too many companies. Indeed most other multinational companies operating in Nigeria also remained silent about human rights violations.

Sir Geoffrey Chandler says the days when companies could remain silent about human rights issues are over: 'Silence or inaction will be seen to provide comfort to oppression and may be adjudged complicity....Silence is not neutrality. To do nothing is not an option.'[103]

John Elkington agrees:

The worst blind-spot today's business leaders suffer from in this area is the belief that if they can just manage to keep their heads down, they can avoid the sorts of challenges that have buffeted companies like Shell and Texaco. Instead, the evidence increasingly suggests that even companies that normally operate well outside the spotlight – and therefore often have little or no experience of dealing with the new stakeholders and their complex, interlocking agendas – will find themselves inexorably drawn into the wrenching con-troversies....[104]

Louisa Wah, writing in the American Management Association International's *Management Review* in 1998, advised companies that when it comes to human rights issues, 'simply avoiding bad press or side-stepping the issue is not enough....'[105]

The Economist noted in December 1998:

Today multinationals are under pressure as never before to justify their dealings with abusive regimes and their treatment of employees in developing countries. Firms used to brush off criticism, saying that they had no control over third-world suppliers, and that politics was none of their business anyway. This is no longer good enough.[106]

2.2 A more sceptical and demanding public

Companies are realising that their credibility with the public has been strained in recent years, and that in a dispute with a human rights organisation or an environmental organisation they cannot depend on public opinion to give them the benefit of the doubt...in fact, just the reverse.

Robert Reich, former U.S. Secretary of Labor, recently identified some of the reasons that companies are so concerned about their public image:

Most companies are concerned about their public images because they sell their products directly or indi-rectly to the public; indeed, companies spend billions of dollars each year burnishing their public images. Anything that tarnishes that image may result in lost sales, and also may make it more difficult for the com-pany to receive permits, subsidies, or other discre-tionary benefits from government.[107]

In the aftermath of the Brent Spar affair (the 1995 controversy surrounding Shell's proposed deep-sea disposal of an oil installation), a MORI-conducted poll reflecting public opinion in seven West European countries showed the fol-lowing levels of confidence in statements about the environment: 27% confidence in statements by the oil industry (in Spain and Germany the level was closer to 10%), 29% confidence in gov-ernment statements, 63% confidence in state-ments by environmental groups, and 65% confi-dence in statements by academics.[108]

Royal Dutch/Shell, in its 1998 social report, noted:

Multinationals have been criticised as being overly concerned with profit and failing to take their broad-er responsibilities seriously: to defend human rights, to protect the environment, to be good corporate citizens. [This debate] is taking place in a fast-changing world, characterised by global communications and diminishing respect for established authority.... [P]eople are withdrawing their trust in traditional institutions unless it can be demonstrated that such faith is warranted — what has been called a move from a 'trust me' to a 'show me' world.[109]

Some segments of the public are extremely scep-tical about the entire notion of the business community getting serious about human rights. They see companies as part of the human rights problem internationally, rather than part of the solution. Some of these sceptics have first-hand knowledge of human rights abuses in which a company was directly or indirectly involved, and they have great difficulty trusting the intentions of that company or the private sector in general.

Many others see business capable of both harm and good in the human rights sphere. Twenty years ago most of these people probably would have given business the benefit of the doubt in a human rights controversy. But that is no longer the case. In the past two decades they have been disappointed too many times by dis-closures about the human rights record of par-ticular companies. While they welcome news that a company has adopted a human rights policy, they now withhold judgement to see whether the company follows through with action, and whether the results have been veri-fied by an organisation truly independent of the company and without any motive to sugar-coat the findings. Too often they have seen companies only address human rights issues when forced to do so by public exposure. They have seen too many companies respond with approaches that are superficial, minimalist, and short-term, looking more like a slick public rela-tions exercise than a genuine commitment to improving the human rights situation. They have heard too many companies say they believe in constructive engagement and 'quiet diplomacy' on human rights issues, in situations where there is little or no evidence that such engagement or diplomacy is actually taking place. They have heard too many companies say they cannot act alone to promote human rights because that might disadvantage them vis-a-vis their competitors. These companies often suggest that action on human rights be taken collectively through an industry association or chamber of commerce, but such organisations too often adopt a lowest-common-denominator approach to human rights issues, doing as much in the human rights sphere as their least courageous members (i.e., they often do nothing at all).

Peter Sutherland, former Director-General of the World Trade Organization, says: 'Business must re-establish trust with society. That will be done by example, not just talking.....It is right that business is scrutinised and that good business is rewarded with praise while bad business is punished with exposure.'[110]

Many companies have underestimated the ability of the public to see through company initiatives that are less than thorough in addressing human rights issues. The public and media no longer accept assurances from business about environmental and social issues — they want factual answers and verifiable commitments.

2.3 The informed consumer

In a 1993 survey of over 1500 households in the U.S., 76.8% of respondents said that a company's community relations activities make a difference in determining whether or not they do business with it. 74% of respondents said they deliberately chose not to buy products from companies they thought had failed to act in the best interests of the community.[111]

In a 1995 survey in the U.S., 78% of respondents said they would prefer to shop at retail stores that had committed themselves to ending apparel worker abuse; 84% said they would pay an extra $1 on a $20 item to ensure that the garment had been made in a worker-friendly environment.[112]

A garment industry consultant writing in the *Wall Street Journal* acknowledged that consumers are increasingly taking human rights issues into account:

What's changed is that for the first time human rights concerns could become a major marketing issue and tool for manufacturers. In an era when companies must work harder than ever to sell their products, anything that turns the consumer off has to be avoided at all costs....I am not speaking as a do-gooder....I am a garment industry consultant who has spent 30 years in Asia showing companies how to produce and buy better garments for less money. And I know for a fact that no social adjustments take place in the world of business unless the cost-accountants prove that change is necessary. But I am here to tell you that the tapping noise you hear on your door is your CPA [certified public accountant] coming to announce that something is indeed happening out there, and that if you want to survive, now would be a good time to develop a social conscience....

[T]ake Burma, where orders for exported garments produced by Burmese factories have fallen by two-thirds over the past year. Companies like Eddie Bauer, Liz Claiborne and Federated Department Stores, which in the past found some of their best bargains in Burma, are now discovering that in today's socially conscious marketplace these products are less competitive. You may ask, 'What does Aung San Suu Kyi have to do with fashion?' The latest answer is, 'A lot.'[113]

In the U.S., recent grassroots consumer campaigns targeting companies doing business in Burma have been cited as important factors in some of those companies withdrawing from Burma. PepsiCo announced its complete withdrawal from Burma after Harvard University turned down Pepsi for a $1 million contract and Stanford University decided not to allow Taco Bell (a PepsiCo restaurant) on campus after 2000 students petitioned the university to sever ties with all companies doing business in Burma.[114]

A 1995 survey of 30,000 people in the U.K. by the Gallup Organization and Co-operative Bank showed that 60% were more worried about shopping ethics than they were five years before. 60% said they would pay up to 7% more for goods meeting ethical standards.[115] In the early 1990s the Co-operative Bank launched an advertising campaign in the U.K. drawing attention to its policy of not investing in countries with a very poor human rights record. This campaign reportedly was instrumental in bringing in tens of thousands of customers who opened more than 1000 accounts per week.[116]

A 1995 study carried out on behalf of a Canadian labour union indicated that over 92% of Canadians would choose to buy products made ethically if given a choice between an 'ethical' and a 'regular' product. 89% said they would pay more for clothing produced under ethical conditions and over two-thirds would be more likely to shop in a store selling ethical products.[117]

2.4 Intergovernmental organisations

International human rights instruments make clear that while human rights accountability is focused on governments, individuals and social institutions (including companies) have responsibilities to promote respect for human rights. The Universal Declaration of Human Rights, adopted by the U.N. General Assembly in 1948, states in its preamble that 'every individual and every organ of society, keeping this Declaration constantly in mind, shall strive by teaching and education to promote respect for these rights and freedoms and by progressive measures, national and international, to secure their universal and effective recognition and observance....'[118] The International Covenant on Civil and Political Rights, and the International Covenant on Economic, Social and Cultural Rights, adopted by the U.N. General Assembly in 1966, both include the following statement in their preambles: '[T]he individual...is under a responsibility to strive for the promotion and observance of the rights recognized in the present Covenant.'[119]

U.N. Secretary-General Kofi Annan, speaking at the Davos World Economic Forum in January 1999, called on multinational companies to promote universal values in their dealings, and to 'uphold human rights and decent labour and environmental standards directly, by your own conduct of your own business.'[120] He has proposed a 'Global Compact', challenging business leaders to abide by nine principles derived from internationally-recognised standards:

Human rights

1. *Business should support and respect the protection of internationally proclaimed human rights within their sphere of influence; and*
2. *make sure they are not complicit in human rights abuses.*

Labour

3. *Businesses should uphold the freedom of association and the effective recognition of the right to collective bargaining;*
4. *the elimination of all forms of forced and compulsory labour;*
5. *the effective abolition of child labour; and*
6. *eliminate discrimination in respect of employment and occupation.*

Environment

7. *Businesses should support a precautionary approach to environmental challenges;*
8. *undertake initiatives to promote greater environmental responsibility; and*
9. *encourage the development and diffusion of environmentally friendly technologies.*[121]

The U.N. fact sheet explaining the Global Compact with business notes: 'Although governments have primary responsibility for implementing internationally accepted values, corporations acting on their own can do a great deal to actualize these principles within their spheres of influence.'[122] The U.N. says that supporting the nine principles of the Global Compact is the right thing to do and is also good for business: 'A clear demonstration that basic and broadly popular social values are being advanced as part and parcel of the globalization process will help ensure that markets remain open, and will truly bring the people of the world closer together.'[123] On 5 July 1999 U.N. Secretary-General Annan and the President of the International Chamber of Commerce (and other business leaders representing the ICC) issued a joint statement stating that 'business leaders welcomed the United Nations Secretary-General's call for a Global Compact between the United Nations and the private sector to promote human rights, improve labour conditions – and protect the environment.'[124]

Mary Robinson, U.N. High Commissioner for Human Rights, in June 1999 delivered a speech on the subject of business and human rights in which she noted that 'civil society is scrutinizing corporate conduct much as it has watched the behavior of Governments in the past.' She welcomed the fact that a number of business people were recognising 'that the long term viability of their corporate activities and the future protection of shareholder value will be enhanced if the countries they are involved with respect human rights.' She added: 'The rights in the Universal Declaration [of Human Rights] contribute, both directly and indirectly, to the social and political conditions conducive to business.' She encouraged companies to integrate human rights concerns into every aspect of their business in a meaningful way: 'Human rights are not an 'add on', they should be central to companies' approach to investment and doing business.' Finally, the High Commissioner said that her office and other U.N. agencies would be happy 'to assist the private sector in incorporating the agreed values and principles into mission statements and corporate practices'.[125]

When the U.N. General Assembly adopted the Declaration on the Right to Development in 1986, it made clear that the responsibility to promote development does not apply only to governments:

All human beings have a responsibility for development, individually and collectively, taking into account the need for full respect for their human rights and fundamental freedoms as well as their duties to the community, which alone can ensure the free and complete fulfilment of the human being, and they should therefore promote and protect an appropriate political, social and economic order for development.[126]

The U.N. Declaration on the Right to Development says that development should promote 'a new international economic order based on sovereign equality, interdependence, mutual interest and cooperation among all States as well as to encourage the observance and realization of human rights.'[127]

In 1999 the U.N. Commission on Human Rights requested the U.N. Sub-Commission on Prevention of Discrimination and Protection of Minorities to undertake a study on the issue of globalisation and its impact on the full enjoyment of human rights.[128] The Sub-Commission has appointed one of its members to prepare this study, which will be presented to the Commission at its meeting in 2001.[129]

In 1998 the Sub-Commission decided to form a working group for a three-year period to examine the activities of transnational corporations from a human rights perspective.[130] At that working group's first session in August 1999, individual Sub-Commission members volunteered to draft:

i) a code of conduct for transnational corporations based on human rights standards;

ii) a proposal for a mechanism for the implementation of a code of conduct;

iii) a compilation and analysis of relevant human rights standards; and

iv) a paper on the identification and examination of the effects of the activities of transnational corporations on the enjoyment of human rights.[131]

The Sub-Commission plans to hold during its year 2000 session a three-day 'Forum on Economic, Social and Cultural Rights,' to analyse violations of economic, social and cultural rights and their relation to globalisation.[132]

At the Sub-Commission's 1999 session it adopted a resolution requesting 'all Governments and economic policy forums to take international human rights obligations and principles fully into account in international policy formulation'.[133]

At the 1995 U.N. World Summit for Social Development (Copenhagen), governments reached consensus on the principle that respect for human rights is necessary for sustainable development.[134] The World Summit agreed that the private sector should be one of the actors involved in taking steps to address social development issues,[135] and stated:

Making economic growth and the interaction of market forces more conducive to social development requires the following actions: …Encouraging transnational and national corporations to operate in a framework of respect for the environment while complying with national laws and legislation, and in accordance with international agreements and conventions, and with proper consideration for the social and cultural impact of their activities....[136]

The 1977 International Labour Organization (ILO) 'Tripartite Declaration of Principles Concerning Multinational Enterprises and Social Policy' states in its introduction that multinational corporations can 'make an important contribution to the promotion of economic and social welfare' and 'to the enjoyment of basic human rights'.[137] But it notes that they can also abuse their power by operating in a way that conflicts with the workers' and country's best interests.[138] It says the aim of the Tripartite Declaration is 'to encourage the positive contribution which multinational enterprises can make to economic and social progress and to minimize and resolve the difficulties to which their various operations may give rise.'[139] It also says all the parties concerned by the declaration (governments, employers and workers) 'should respect the Universal Declaration of Human Rights and the corresponding International Covenants adopted by the General Assembly of the United Nations as well as the Constitution of the International Labour Organization and its principles according to which freedom of expression and association are essential to sustained progress.'[140]

The ILO, through its 1998 'ILO Declaration on fundamental principles and rights at work' and its public statements, has been emphasising to governments and the private sector that 'in a situation of growing economic interdependence' it is important to promote worldwide respect for fundamental principles such as freedom of association, the right to collective bargaining, the elimination of forced labour, the abolition of child labour, and the elimination of discrimination in employment.[141]

The 'OECD Guidelines for Multinational Enterprises' were adopted in 1976 and last revised in 1991 when a section on environmental protection was added; the entire set of guidelines is currently under review. The introduction to the OECD Guidelines states: 'The common aim of Member countries is to encourage the positive contributions which multinational enterprises can make to economic and

social progress and to minimise and resolve the difficulties to which their various operations may give rise....with a view to improving the welfare and living standards of all people.'[142] The Guidelines include a section on 'Employment and industrial relations,' and say that multinational enterprises should, *inter alia*:

[G]ive due consideration to those countries' [the countries in which they operate] aims and priorities with regard to economic and social progress, including industrial and regional development, the protection of the environment and consumer interests, the creation of employment opportunities, the promotion of innovation and the transfer of technology;...

Favour close co-operation with the local community and business interests;...[143]

A May 1995 OECD Development Assistance Committee policy statement ('Development Partnerships in the New Global Context') says that a key element to the success of sustainable development is: 'Good governance and public management, democratic accountability, the protection of human rights and the rule of law.'[144] The statement also says: 'Development and greater interdependence require high levels of domestic effort, high standards of accountability, and a strong civil society....More widespread and sustainable progress now depends on building strong capacities to achieve good governance, reduce poverty, and protect the environment.'[145]

A May 1996 statement by the OECD Development Assistance Committee ('Shaping the 21st Century: The Contribution of Development Co-operation') says that governments have a responsibility to 'open up wide scope for effective development contributions from throughout civil society.'[146] The statement notes:

Partnerships are becoming more complex. Earlier aid efforts involved working almost always with central governments. Today, we are working with many more partners to meet demands for greater efficiency, respond to more pluralistic and decentralised political systems, and recognise the importance of a dynamic private sector, local ownership and participation by civil society. Our understanding of development and development co-operation has undergone fundamental change....We now see a much broader range of aims for a more people-centred, participatory and sustainable development process.[147]

The European Parliament in January 1999 passed a resolution, 'Code of conduct for European enterprises operating in developing countries,' that, *inter alia*:

i) encourages company codes of conduct 'with effective and independent monitoring and verification, and stakeholder participation in the development, implementation and monitoring of these codes';

ii) recommends that a model Code of Conduct for European businesses should be adopted, guaranteeing minimum internationally-recognised standards on the environment, health and safety conditions in the workplace, and respect for basic human rights; and

iii) requests the European Commission to establish an independent body of experts to monitor and verify implementation of the Code of Conduct, identify best practices, and receive complaints about corporate conduct from interested parties.[148]

Richard Howitt, the MEP (Member of European Parliament) from the U.K. who introduced the resolution, said:

What I want to emphasise is that our proposal is not to draw up a different set of standards just for Europe. Our purpose is to adopt a series of minimum applicable international standards which have been agreed already within bodies such as the United Nations and the International Labour Organisation, and to use the European Union to promote their implementation and to monitor those standards....[M]any people from developing countries, as well as trade unionists, have said that when new codes of business practice are drawn up, they often involve dilution of standards which have been negotiated over many years within international institutions. This proposal is intended to avoid such dilution.[149]

2.5 Governments

In the U.K., both the Foreign & Commonwealth Office (FCO) and the Department for International Development (DFID) have established units to promote and support socially responsible business. Alastair Newton, Head of the FCO's new Global Citizenship Unit, commented: 'Corporate Social Responsibility is now evolving into what promises to be one of the big issues of the next decade.'[150] The FCO says that through its network of embassies it can help British companies uphold high standards of corporate citizenship. DFID set up a Business Partnership Unit in 1997 to coordinate its approach to working in partnership with the private sector. DFID considers that companies can play an important role in poverty eradication, and it tries to promote the developmental aspects of business in developing countries. DFID routinely consults the private sector about development issues and when it develops its Country Strategy Papers.[151] DFID's recently-published *Partnerships with Business* says:

The 'triple-bottom line' acknowledges that sustainable competitive advantage now requires companies to be economically viable, environmentally sound and socially responsible. This makes strong business sense: for example, decent and equitable employment conditions make a more committed and productive workforce; social investment in host communities widens a business's understanding of the local situation and market conditions and, in the information age, customers are demanding it.[152]

The Government of the Netherlands recently emphasised (in an explanatory memorandum to the 1998 budget of the Netherlands Ministry of Foreign Affairs) that it is important for multinational corporations to remain alert to the human rights situation in countries where they operate and to ensure that their activities do not contribute to a continuation of human rights violations. The memorandum also says corporations should contribute to the creation of an enabling environment for the realisation of human rights.[153]

In the U.S., the White House announced in May 1995 the 'Model Business Principles,' a one-page voluntary code of human rights principles for U.S. companies operating abroad.[154] This document refers to principles including 'provision of a safe and healthy workplace,' 'fair employment practices, including avoidance of child and forced labour and avoidance of dis-crimination,' 'responsible environmental pro-tection,' and freedom of expression. Companies were encouraged to include these principles in their voluntary codes of conduct. The 'Model Business Principles' have been crit-icised by human rights advocates for being too vague, incomplete in terms of the substantive rights included, and lacking a framework for effective implementation.[155] It was reported in 1997 that relatively little had been done since 1995 by the U.S. Government to promote these principles.[156]

In 1996 President Clinton appointed the Apparel Industry Partnership (see section 3.4 of this report).

The Canadian Government convened a meeting in May 1999 of Canadian retailers, manufacturers and NGOs to discuss how to ensure that consumer products sold in Canada are made under humane working conditions. The participants agreed to form a joint working group to develop a Canadian basic code of labour practice.[157]

South African President Nelson Mandela has called on the business community to contribute to social development:

There are many ways in which the special skills and know-how of the business community can help the government achieve its development objectives;[158]

Development can no longer be regarded as the respon-sibility of government alone. It requires a partnership of government with its social partners: private sector, labour and non-governmental organisations.[159]

2.6 Non-governmental organisations (NGOs)

Amnesty International's *Human Rights Principles for Companies* (and accompanying *Introductory Checklist*)[160] contain standards on the following subjects:

i) Personnel practices and policies;

ii) Security arrangements;

iii) Responsibility for promoting and uphold-ing human rights standards;

iv) Implementation and monitoring;

v) Company policy on human rights;

vi) Community engagement;

vii) Prohibition of forced labour, bonded child labour, coerced prison labour;

viii) Health and safety;

ix) Freedom of association and the right to col-lective bargaining; and

x) Fair working conditions.

Amnesty International, in spite of having a more limited mandate than most other human rights organisations, is increasingly addressing business issues in its country reports. It has always addressed human rights violations directed against workers and trade unionists in its reports, and continues to do so. There is increasing attention to identifying links between companies and human rights con-cerns. For example, in late 1996 Amnesty International published a report on Nigeria that includes a section entitled 'Transnational companies.'[161]

Amnesty International is also increasingly integrating a business component into its human rights promotion initiatives: challeng-ing the business community to play a more active and constructive role in addressing human rights issues. For example, during the organisation's 1996 campaign on China it issued a special set of papers for business peo-ple, entitled 'Human rights are everybody's business.'[162] The papers included an explana-tion of Amnesty International's concerns in China, recommended steps for companies operating in China to promote human rights, and articles written by business people about the importance of the private sector's support for human rights.

Sir Geoffrey Chandler, Chairperson of Amnesty International's U.K. Section Business Group, emphasises that the Universal Declaration of Human Rights 'not only legit-imises a company's right to speak out on such matters; it imposes an obligation to do so.'[163] He recently commented, in a *Time* magazine guest editorial distributed to participants in the 1999 Davos World Economic Forum, that cor-porations must change their perception 'about the frontiers of their responsibility.' They must recognise that 'they bear responsibility for the total impact of their operations – for the man-ner in which they treat their employees, for their security arrangements, for their effect on the social, physical and political environment in which they operate.'[164]

Human Rights Watch, in its 'Working Guidelines on Business and Human Rights,'[165] explains that its research and advocacy is focused on three issues where companies have been complicit in human rights abuses or have gained advantage from human rights abuses:

i) Direct corporate complicity;

ii) Corporate advantage from the failure of government enforcement; and

iii) Inappropriate corporate presence.

The Human Rights Watch guidelines include a section on 'Proactive Measures,' that says:

Human Rights Watch urges corporations to be a force for improving respect for human rights through a broad range of actions, including:

* emphasizing commitment to the rule of law which underlies respect of human rights;

* protesting restrictions on civil and political rights, for example freedom of expression, association or assembly;

* using influence with governments to raise concerns about human rights violations;

* respecting and protecting the basic human rights, including labor rights, of their employees.

The Human Rights Watch guidelines conclude with the following statement:

In countries characterized by severe human rights violations, corporations often justify their presence by arguing that their operations will enhance respect for rights but then adopt no substantive measures to achieve that end. Corporations doing business in these states take on a special obligation to implement proactive steps to promote respect for rights and to ensure that they do not become complicit in rights violations. Where a corporation uses 'constructive engagement' to justify its presence in such a country, we will examine whether it has taken any of the acts listed above.

Human Rights Watch has also been giving more attention to the human rights-related record of corporations in its country reports. In 1996 it published *Mexico – No Guarantees: Sex Discrimination in Mexico's Maquiladora Sector*, which examined discrimination against and mistreatment of women workers in export-processing factories owned by multinationals.[166] That report was updated in a 1998 report: *Mexico – A Job or Your Rights: Continued Sex Discrimination in Mexico's Maquiladora Sector.*[167] In 1998 Human Rights Watch published *Colombia: Human rights concerns raised by the security arrangements of transnational oil companies.*[168] That report includes recommendations to oil companies aimed at preventing further human rights violations by military forces protecting company interests in Colombia, and letters from Human Rights Watch to BP and to Occidental Petroleum.

In January 1999 Human Rights Watch published two books that examine in great detail the human rights-related record of corporations:

i) *The Enron Corporation: Corporate Complicity in Human Rights Violations*[169] focuses on the Dabhol Power Corporation (DPC), an Indian subsidiary of Houston-based Enron Corporation. The Dabhol Power project in the State of Maharashtra constitutes the largest single foreign investment in India. The Human Rights Watch report examines the complex history of this project from its inception in 1992, particularly the local opposition that arose from environmental activists and villagers' organisations, and human rights violations including suppression of freedom of expression and peaceful assembly, arbitrary detention, and excessive use of force by the police. The report states that DPC was complicit in these violations because it:

• paid the police security forces located adjacent to the project site;

• did not adequately investigate complaints that DPC contractors committed abuses; and

• did not speak out about human rights violations.

The report identifies the interconnected responsibility of all the actors in this project for the human rights violations that occurred: the Government of India, the State Government of Maharashtra, the Enron Corporation, the U.S. Government ('the U.S. government bears special responsibility because…it extended hundreds of millions of dollars in public funds for the project while seemingly indifferent [to] human rights-related conditionalities that apply to such transactions'),[170] and public and private financial institutions that financed the project.

ii) *The Price of Oil: Corporate Responsibility and Human Rights Violations in Nigeria's Oil Producing Communities*[171] examines in considerable detail the connection between international oil companies and human rights violations in the oil-producing region of Nigeria. It includes recommendations to the Nigerian Government, the international oil companies operating in Nigeria, and the international community.

In May 1999 Global Exchange and the International Labor Rights Fund (ILRF) launched a set of 'US Business Principles for Human Rights of Workers in China,' a 10-point code of conduct based on internationally-recognised human rights of workers. Since then a number of human rights organisations have endorsed the principles, and three companies (Levi Strauss & Co., Mattel and Reebok) reportedly have announced that they will sign the principles.[172]

At the 1993 U.N. World Conference on Human Rights (Vienna), more than 1000 NGOs from all regions of the world participated in an NGO Forum that adopted in its 'NGO Forum Final Report' recommendations including the following:

Urgent and effective steps must be taken to ensure that multinational corporations and other non-State violators of human rights are subjected to the standards and obligations of international human rights law.

The Working Group proposes… Accountability of major institutions of society, in terms of their obligations nationally and internationally, ie States, multinational corporations, global financial and other institutions, religious bodies, big national and international non-governmental organizations, in terms of the principle that parallel to the universality of rights lies the universality of accountability of all institutions.[173]

The Interfaith Center on Corporate Responsibility (U.S.), The Ecumenical Council for Corporate Responsibility (U.K./Ireland) and The Taskforce on the Churches and Corporate Responsibility (Canada) together developed *Principles for Global Corporate Responsibility: Bench Marks for Measuring Business Performance.*[174] These principles, adopted in 1995 and revised in 1998, say that a responsible company has the following characteristics:

The company is fully committed to respecting internationally recognized human rights standards, including the Universal Declaration of Human Rights.…

In instances where legislation or the actual practices of any public institution violate fundamental human rights, the company does everything in its power to maintain respect for those fundamental rights in its own operations. The company also seeks to exercise its corporate influence to contribute to the establishment of such fundamental rights.

The company has a policy that it will withdraw from a country in instances where there are gross and systematic violations of human rights and when there is a recognized movement from within the country calling for withdrawal.

An active human rights committee has been established by and reports to the Board of Directors.

A senior executive in each operation is responsible for all matters of human rights.[175]

New York-based Council on Economic Priorities (CEP) in 1997 launched SA8000, a social accountability code providing global standards on workers' rights including trade union rights, child labour, forced labour, compensation, and health and safety (see section 3.4 for further details).[176] CEP's research team tracks hundreds of corporations internationally, rating their performance on issues including the environment, women's advancement, minority advancement, charitable giving, community outreach, family benefits, workplace issues, disclosure of information, military contracts, and animal testing. CEP uses this information in its SCREEN and GLOBAL SCREEN services for investors, in its *Shopping for a Better World* guide for consumers, and in other publications such as its 1998 book *The Corporate Report Card: Rating*

250 of America's Corporations for the Socially Responsible Investor.[177] The CEP's annual Corporate Conscience Awards have included an award for the category 'International Human Rights.'[178]

World Monitors, a New York-based firm providing consulting services to multinational corporations seeking to develop and implement socially responsible business policies, publishes a regular on-line newsletter to keep subscribers informed of developments concerning business and human rights.[179]

In 1995 Robert MacGregor, President of the Minnesota Center for Corporate Responsibility (which initiated the 'The Caux Round Table Principles for Business,' described in section 3.1 of this report), made the following comment at an International Anti-Corruption Conference in Beijing where Chinese President Jiang Zemin was the principal speaker: 'In business, 80 per cent of success has to do with financial matters, but 20 per cent has to do with values. If the 20 per cent is out of whack, the whole system will end up going down, and stable business relationships and a sustainable world community will be impossible.'[180]

The California Global Corporate Accountability Project, launched in January 1999, aims 'to enhance the standards of U.S. multinationals in terms of both environmental protection and promotion of human rights.'[181] The two-year project will monitor the overseas performance of multinationals headquartered in California in three industry sectors: oil, technology and finance. It will focus on whether or not corporations are abiding by environmental standards, human rights standards, and their own codes of conduct. The project will consider what mechanisms could enhance the monitoring and regulation of corporate conduct. It will also encourage a network of environmental and human rights NGOs to work together on these issues, and will operate an on-line corporate accountability documentation center.[182]

The International Centre for Human Rights and Democratic Development (ICHRDD) in Canada has given much attention to the subject of business and human rights in its publications and conferences. Ed Broadbent, when he was the organisation's president in 1996, identified

three practical steps that companies can take to address human rights:

i) adopt codes of conduct aimed at ensuring that business operations respect international human rights principles;

ii) integrate information about human rights as part of strategic research prior to business trips and use whatever opportunities are available to inquire about such matters with local authorities; and

iii) establish a charitable fund for human rights groups with a percentage of corporate profits.[183]

Warren Allmand, ICHRDD's president in 1997, said:

[B]usinesses have an important role to play, not only in actively promoting human rights, but in ensuring that business as usual does not contribute to human rights abuses. Businesses must be particularly wary that their presence does not induce regimes that abuse human rights to increase their repressive activity or insulate such regimes from democratization.[184]

The Ethical Trading Initiative in the U.K. is 'an alliance of companies, non-governmental organisations (NGOs) and trade union organisations committed to working together to identify and promote good practice in the implementation of codes of labour practice, including the monitoring and independent verification of the observance of code provisions.'[185]

Development organisations such as Oxfam, Christian Aid, Save the Children and ActionAid during the 1990s have given increasing attention to the links between civil/political rights and economic/social/cultural rights. Oxfam emphasised at the 1993 U.N. World Conference on Human Rights 'the view, based on experience of working with poor people throughout the developing world, that poverty tends to be characterized not only by material insufficiency but also by denial of rights....Political participation and economic empowerment, it believes, can be shown to be essential elements in all successful development programmes.'[186]

The 1998 Quito Declaration (on the enforcement and realization of economic, social and cultural rights in Latin America and the Caribbean), adopted by more than 50 development and human rights NGOs, says:

States have the primary obligation of respecting, pro-
tecting, and promoting ESCR [economic, social and
cultural rights] before the international community
and their citizens. Nevertheless, other actors such as
multinational corporations and multilateral organi-
zations also have the duty to respect these rights and
are accountable to them. Because of this, civil society
as much as the international community and the
States, when confronted with violations by deed or
omission committed by actors such as multinational
corporations and/or multilateral agencies, should
adopt, individually or by means of international
cooperation, effective measures to prevent and sanc-
tion violations of these rights.[187]

The Quito Declaration also includes the following appeals 'to multinational and national companies':

That they adopt social ethics guidelines and codes of
conduct that ensure the harmonization of their activ-
ities with their duty to respect all human rights.

That they scrupulously respect the standards of the
ILO regarding the promotion and protection of the
fundamental rights of workers.

That they take responsibility, including legal respon-
sibility, for their actions and the impacts of these
actions, relating to the ESCR [economic, social and
cultural rights] of their workers, the users and con-
sumers of their products or services, and/or the popu-
lations generally affected by their productive or com-
mercial practices.

That they allow independent oversight and/or regu-
lar monitoring by civil society over those actions of an
economic, social and/or cultural nature.[188]

Chris Jochnick, The Advocacy Director for the
Center for Economic and Social Rights (an
NGO established in 1993 to encourage respect
for those rights[189]), wrote in 1999 that the 'regulation of TNCs [transnational corporations] is
perhaps the most pressing task for the promotion of ESCR [economic, social and cultural
rights]….TNCs exercise an inordinate influence over local laws and policies. Their impact
on human rights ranges from a direct role in
violations, such as abuses of employees or the

environment, to indirect support of governments guilty of widespread repression.'[190]

Development agencies are giving increasing
attention to encouraging business to contribute
positively to sustainable development and
human rights. They urge companies:

i)   to avoid harm to the well-being of local
     communities;

ii) to use their influence with governmental
     authorities to press for funds (for example,
     fees paid by the company for joint ventures
     or exploration rights) to be used in ways
     that promote sustainable development for
     local communities and for others in need;

iii) to work in partnership with local commu-
     nities and NGOs to contribute positively to
     sustainable development, poverty allevia-
     tion, education, health care, and other
     social needs.

For example, ActionAid works with companies on development projects aimed at eradi-
cating poverty. In India ActionAid supports
Partners in Change, an organisation that builds
'meaningful and sustainable partnership
between socially responsible companies and disadvantaged communities, both directly and
through effective NGOs.'[191] Partners in Change
helps companies (multinationals operating in
India and Indian companies) develop a social
development policy, identify NGO partners,
sensitise and train company staff on social
development issues, and monitor the progress
of social development programmes.[192]

Accountable Aid,[193] an Oxfam study of major
development programmes in Brazil, India and
Uganda, sets forth six principles for accountable development derived from internationally-
recognised human rights standards that Oxfam
says should be respected by companies as well
as governments, international financial institutions and NGOs:

i)   **Due diligence**: 'Donors or private agents
     have an obligation to exercise due care
     before undertaking a project or investment
     operation. This means, among other
     things, examining and taking into account
     the political, social and environmental con-
     text; consulting widely with representatives
     of civil society…; and ensuring that donors
     are aware of the most recent human rights
     reports on the public record.'

ii) **Non-discrimination**: 'Donors have an obligation to ensure that development initiatives do not increase divisions in a recipient country, for example between ethnic groups, or otherwise contribute to perpetuating discriminatory practices....'

iii) **Advisability**: 'Multilateral agencies, donors, or other private agents should respect the provision of the International Covenant on Economic, Social and Cultural Rights, which emphasises the need to ensure that development co-operation activities enhance the ability of recipient governments to promote economic and social rights, including the rights to an adequate standard of living, and to access to education, and the best possible level of health care....'

iv) **Participation**: 'International human-rights standards have long recognised the right of individuals and communities to be involved in the formulation and implementation of policies, programmes, budgets, legislation, and other activities....It is recognised that effective participation requires access to information about development and environmental initiatives held by public authorities or donors or even private companies.'

v) **Accountability**: 'Donors, private companies, and governments have a duty to accept responsibility for their actions. This requires them to be transparent in their undertakings and honest in the presentation of operations to civil society and stakeholders. It means that they must take particular care to consult with local communities and to keep them informed during implementation of specific projects and programmes. It also requires them to be prepared to submit their operations to independent scrutiny and oversight. Where changes have to be made to programmes or operations, they should be based, as far as possible, on consensus. However, additional measures may have to be taken to protect the rights and interests of vulnerable groups. If problems arise, it is unacceptable for donors and private companies to simply withdraw from engagement.'

vi) **Redress**: '...Most of the multilateral agencies have followed the World Bank's example and set up complaints mechanisms, but obtaining effective and timely remedial action when development initiatives cause harm to local people is still a protracted and thankless process. With the privatisation of development, it is even more urgent for private companies to ensure that credible dispute-settlement mechanisms are put in place at the outset of their operations. Donors and companies need to ensure that there is a fair process for adjudicating legitimate claims, given the difficulties – political, financial and cultural – that confront poor communities when they try to gain access to the courts.'[194]

2.7 Non-governmental organisations and companies begin engaging

Human rights organisations are increasingly engaging directly with business people (and vice versa) about the human rights responsibilities of business. Sir Geoffrey Chandler, who previously worked for Royal Dutch/Shell and now works for Amnesty International, recently noted that there needs to be 'an understanding by both companies and NGOs that neither can fulfil their objectives without the other':[195]

Companies need the expertise of NGOs in tackling problems of which they have inadequate knowledge. NGOs need the huge and growing influence of companies if they are to maximise their impact. Protest may win battles, and is indeed a weapon that cannot be surrendered, but it will not win the war or the argument. For this, dialogue is required. And over the past two years there has been the beginnings of a sea-change as the mutual suspicions, hostility and ignorance of the two sides have given way to tentative engagement on problems in the solution of which both have an interest.[196]

The Fund for Peace, a non-governmental organisation based in Washington, D.C., launched a Foreign Policy Roundtable in January 1998 that brings together on a regular basis corporate and human rights representatives to discuss issues of mutual concern.[197]

In 1998 Amnesty International's Asia-Pacific Program Director was invited to address the Keidanren (Japan Federation of Economic

Organisations), the body that brings together the country's senior business and industrial leaders. Referring to the Asian economic crisis and recent political developments in the region, he said to the Keidanren:

One lesson is clear. The...factors which protect human rights – the rule of law; open, transparent and accountable government; the independence of the judiciary; uncorrupted institutions; freedom of information – are the same factors which underpin sustainable development and a stable business environment. In this way, agendas for the protection of human rights and business interests come together....

I have talked a lot today about the self interest business has in engaging with the human rights agenda. But it goes further than this. Business has a responsibility – moral and legal – to use its influence to promote respect for human rights. The Universal Declaration of Human Rights calls on 'every individual and every organ of society' to join in the task of promoting and protecting the rights enshrined in it. In this globalised world, businesses are among the most powerful organs of society – they share a responsibility for the promotion and protection of human rights with the governments and citizens of the world.[198]

Amnesty International's Secretary General, Pierre Sané, was invited to speak to a 1998 international conference of oil company executives and government ministers responsible for oil and energy. He said in his speech:

It is a company's responsibility to anticipate and provide for human rights problems at any point in its operations in the same way that it has learnt to anticipate environmental problems. Policies need to be explicit and open. Mistakes may still be made, but secretiveness leads to the suspicion that these are at the best carelessness, at worst collusion.[199]

Since 1996 the Dutch Section of Amnesty International has been holding regular 'Round Table' meetings with around ten Netherlands-based multinational corporations, to discuss how business is addressing and should be addressing human rights issues.[200]

When BP launched its first social report[201] in 1998 it sent copies to a large number of human rights and development organisations and invited them to its London headquarters for a half-day meeting to discuss the report with BP managers. At the outset BP announced that the meeting's purpose was for BP managers to listen rather than talk, and it invited all the representatives of organisations to speak about what they saw as the strengths and weaknesses of the social report, and to give suggestions on how BP could do better in future. BP has also increased its level of engagement with NGOs in the various countries of its operations.

Shell's 1999 social report says: 'We work with human rights organisations to help guide our actions. We see this as a continuous process of understanding and improvement.... We are continuing our efforts to engage in more dialogue with communities wherever we operate.'[202]

Indeed it is important that multinational companies do not only focus their efforts on discussions with international human rights/development organisations. Companies need to ensure that there are also ongoing discussions between their national/local operations and national/local human rights and development organisations.

2.8 Selective purchasing laws

A number of selective purchasing laws have been enacted in the U.S. by state and city governments. Most prevent those state and city governments from dealing with companies doing business in Burma (Myanmar) because of the human rights situation in that country. The states with selective purchasing laws on Burma are Massachusetts and Vermont.[203] Over 20 cities have enacted such laws on Burma, starting in 1995 with Berkeley (California), Madison (Wisconsin) and Santa Monica (California), and now including New York City, Los Angeles, Portland, San Francisco and Oakland.[204] Several localities in Australia recently took a similar step.[205] And Burma is not the only target: Berkeley, Oakland and Alameda County adopted selective purchasing laws on Nigeria during the period of military rule in that country, and Berkeley also targets companies doing business in Tibet if their operations have been criticised by the Tibetan government-in-exile.[206]

Multinational corporations might not have been too worried in 1995 when two college towns and Santa Monica passed these selective purchasing laws, but when the state of Massachusetts and some large cities made the move in 1996 it caused shock waves. Corporations including Unocal reportedly stepped up their lobbying against such laws.[207] The corporate anti-sanctions group called USA*Engage started keeping track of state and local selective purchasing laws on its website.[208] The list of states and cities continued to grow longer. University students and others organised boycotts of companies doing business in Burma.[209]

Meanwhile a number of multinational corporations decided to pull out of Burma, including Apple Computer, Philips Electronics, Eastman Kodak, PepsiCo, Atlantic-Richfield, and Hewlett-Packard.[210]

U.S. Secretary of State Madeleine Albright, addressing the National Conference of State Legislatures on 17 April 1998, expressed broad support of selective purchasing laws, saying that she and 'President Clinton recognize the authority of state and local officials to determine their own investment and procurement policies, and the right – indeed their responsibility – to take moral considerations into account as they do so.'[211]

Less than two weeks later the business community decided to do more than lobby against selective purchasing laws. In late April 1998 the National Foreign Trade Council (NFTC) brought a lawsuit in U.S. federal court alleging that the Massachusetts selective purchasing law on Burma was unconstitutional because it infringed on the federal government's exclusive foreign affairs power. The NFTC is a coalition of 580 major U.S. corporations; the organisation says its members account for 70% of all U.S. non-agricultural exports.[212] The NFTC secured a protective order so that it did not have to reveal (except to the judge) the names of the individual companies that were alleging they were harmed by the Massachusetts law; those corporations feared that if they were publicly named they would be subjected to consumer boycotts.[213]

Simon Billenness of Trillium Asset Management (a Boston-based socially responsible investment advisor) criticises the NFTC's case:

[T]he NFTC and its allies fail to explain adequately why only cities and states should be barred from incorporating moral concerns into their choices in the marketplace. After all, consumers are free to boycott companies that violate their moral concerns. Even corporate members of the NFTC, such as Levi Strauss & Co. and Liz Claiborne, are on the record as ending their contracts to buy from Burmese factories because of the military regime's pervasive abuse of human rights.[214]

The European Union (E.U.) submitted an *amicus curiae* brief in the Massachusetts case on the side of the NFTC, arguing that the Massachusetts law should be struck down because it interfered with free trade and foreign relations between the U.S. and E.U.[215] Indeed the E.U. and Japan (concerned that some of their own multinationals were losing business because of selective purchasing laws) had been threatening to bring a formal case against the U.S. in the World Trade Organization if the Massachusetts law was not repealed.[216]

Others filing *amicus curiae* briefs against the Massachusetts law included the U.S. Chamber of Commerce, the National Association of Manufacturers, and the American Petroleum Institute.[217]

The State of Massachusetts argues that its selective purchasing law is constitutional, in part because the U.S. Congress had implicitly permitted the state's law when Congress in 1996 – months after enactment of the Massachusetts Burma Law and similar local laws – imposed economic sanctions on Burma but took no action to pre-empt state and local laws. Massachusetts also argues that it is simply exercising its right to spend its own money as it sees fit in a free market, and that the 'market participant doctrine' (an exception to the Commerce Clause of the U.S. Constitution) grants cities and states considerable leeway when they participate in the marketplace.[218]

An *amicus curiae* brief filed by human rights organisations supporting the State of Massachusetts says: 'International human rights law establishes a recognized standard of public morality endorsed by the federal government and reserved, in large part, for implementation by the states.' The brief says that when the U.S. federal government ratified the U.N. Charter and human rights treaties, it delegated to the states the necessary authority to implement those treaties, and therefore the Massachusetts Burma law is a legitimate response to the human rights record of Burma's military rulers.[219]

In November 1998 the federal district court struck down the Massachusetts law as unconstitutional, on the basis that it violates the federal government's power to regulate foreign affairs.[220] The Attorney General of Massachusetts appealed the ruling. On 22 June 1999 the U.S. Court of Appeals, while agreeing that human rights conditions in Burma are 'deplorable,' upheld the lower court's ruling, finding that the Massachusetts law was unconstitutional on three counts: it interferes with the federal government's foreign policy powers, it impinges upon Congress' powers to regulate foreign trade, and it was pre-empted by the federal sanctions on Burma.[221] Massachusetts Attorney General Tom Reilly has asked the U.S. Supreme Court to review the case;[222] he commented in July 1999: 'This law is about working for basic human rights and it's about a state's right to choose who it does business with. We believe that the Constitution allows the state to apply a broad and principled standard to buying goods and services. I will continue to defend the Massachusetts Burma Law vigorously.'[223] In October 1999 it was reported that 14 states were planning to file an *amicus curiae* brief supporting the State of Massachusetts: 'The states fear they'll be forced to trade with countries run by brutal regimes if the high court upholds a lower court decision striking down the Massachusetts law.'[224] Other groups signing onto briefs supporting the State of Massachusetts included 11 cities and counties, 44 non-governmental organisations and 54 members of Congress from both parties.[225] If the lower court's decision is not overturned by the Supreme Court, selective purchasing laws in states and cities across the U.S. could be affected. Simon Billenness notes that there is much at stake:

At risk is the rich legacy of state and city action that rose to prominence in the campaign against apartheid in South Africa. The NFTC and its corporate backers clearly see the case as an opportunity to obliterate this method of activism. The result would be to dramatically reduce the tools available for American citizens to hold multinational corporations accountable for their actions abroad.[226]

Burma's military government has closely followed the Massachusetts case. A Burmese Government spokesman reportedly said, speaking on condition of anonymity:

We are following the court hearing with much interest because it seems that this is one of the very few cases where states and cities can infringe on the federal government's exclusive foreign affairs power. We always believe that the truth will eventually prevail and hope those states which have imposed sanctions due to incorrect information or misinformation will come to realize the true situation in Burma and redeem themselves before they commit an unrepairable harm to their own respective states.[227]

Meanwhile, human rights advocates are threatening consumer boycotts of certain large corporations (including those on the NFTC board) if they are denied recourse to selective purchasing laws.[228] If selective purchasing laws are no longer an option, more attention will be given by states, cities and universities to divestment of their investments in any companies doing business in Burma. Indeed a Burma divestment bill reportedly was pending before the Massachusetts state legislature in July 1999.[229]

2.9 Lawsuits against companies

Groundbreaking lawsuits have been brought against multinational corporations for alleged misconduct relating to human rights. For example, in the U.S. lawsuits have been filed against Unocal for abuses in Burma, Shell and Chevron for abuses in Nigeria, The Gap and 17 other clothing retailers for abuses in Saipan (a U.S. territory in the Pacific), Nike for abuses in Asian factories (see section 5.2 of this report), and Texaco for abuses in Ecuador.[230]

2.10 Petitions to revoke corporate charters

On 10 September 1998, thirty citizens' organisations and individuals filed a 127-page petition calling on the California Attorney General to revoke the charter of Unocal oil company. The petition said that Unocal had a record of being a 'repeat offender' of environmental, labour and deceptive practices laws, and that through its operations in Burma and Afghanistan (and its links with those governments) it had been complicit in human rights violations in those countries. California law allows the Attorney General to go to court to dissolve a corporation for wrongdoing and to sell its assets to others who will operate in the public interest.[231]

Law professor Robert Benson, the lead attorney for the petition against Unocal, said 'there has to be a point at which corporate repeat offenders are permanently prevented from doing further harm....The state permanently revokes the licenses of hundreds of doctors, lawyers, accountants and others every year – why not corporations?'[232] Richard Grossman, co-founder of the Program on Corporations, Law and Democracy (one of the petitioning groups), said that the courts have 'always held that corporations are artificial entities, 'mere creatures of the state,' and must be summoned to answer to the people for usurpations of power and violations of the public trust such as those repeatedly committed by the Union Oil Company of California [Unocal].'[233]

On 15 September 1998, three business days after the petition against Unocal had been filed, California's Attorney General declined to institute legal proceedings against Unocal.[234] He did not explain the reason for his decision. In April 1999, after a new state Attorney General had been elected, a coalition of nearly 130 groups and individuals (including 50 law professors) filed a similar petition against Unocal; in May the new Attorney General declined to take action against Unocal without explaining his reasons for doing so.[235]

At the end of 1998 Unocal announced that it was withdrawing from the consortium that had planned to build a pipeline across Afghanistan. The *New York Times* wrote about this on 5 December 1998:

The decision was made under the pressure of low world oil prices, feminist groups that assailed Unocal's contact with the Taliban, the fundamentalist Islamic movement that rules Afghanistan, and concern about the presence of the accused terrorist Osama bin Laden in the country. The Feminist Majority Foundation, a Los Angeles group, petitioned the State of California to revoke Unocal's charter, and Mavis Leno, the wife of 'The Tonight Show' host, Jay Leno, attended a company shareholder meeting last June to complain about its dealings with the Taliban.[236]

Moves to revoke corporate charters have been rare in the past, but a few have been successful. In 1976 the Attorney General of California asked a court to dissolve a private water company for allegedly delivering impure water to its customers; in that case the company settled the case, agreeing to sell its assets to a public water company and go out of business. In 1998 New York's Attorney General dissolved the corporate charter of the Council for Tobacco Research (which had been an advocate for the interests of the tobacco industry) after the Council agreed to go out of existence as part of a settlement of litigation against the tobacco industry in other states. New York's newly elected Attorney General, Mark Spitzer, promised during his campaign to be aggressive in revoking the charters of corporations when it is warranted.[237]

Corporate charter revocation laws in the U.S. codify the English common law writ of *quo warranto*, and therefore charter revocation may be a potential remedy available in other countries as well.[238]

2.11 Shareholder resolutions and annual meetings

Shareholder resolutions about social issues rarely succeed in terms of being approved by a majority of shareholders, but they do draw attention to social issues and add to the pressure on companies. Tim Smith of New York-based Interfaith Center on Corporate Responsibility, an association of nearly 275 Protestant, Roman Catholic and Jewish institutional investors, says that the face-to-face meetings and discussions he holds with companies as a result of shareholder proposals are far more important than the referendum and voting results.[239]

Shareholder proposals on human rights issues have also led to shareholder questions at corporate annual meetings and demonstrations outside those meetings, frustrating company managers by putting them on the defensive in a forum that they intended to be an orchestrated showcase of their company's achievements. A 1998 article noted two examples of such influence:

At the company's May 14 [1998] annual meeting, Mobil Chairman Lucio Noto stated that he would bring up with the Nigerian military junta the cases of two imprisoned oil workers union leaders: Milton Dabibi and Frank Kokori. This statement came in response to a tearful question directed to Mr. Noto by Cordelia Kokori, Frank Kokori's daughter. Both union leaders have since been freed as Nigeria's new military rulers have released nearly all political prisoners.

On August 11 [1998], ARCO announced that it would completely withdraw from Burma. The company maintained that it was pulling out for business reasons only. However, it is clear that the escalating campaign simply wore down the company and that ARCO's Chairman, Mike Bowlin, was fed up by the way in which Burma dominated the company's annual meetings.[240]

A 1996 survey of 100 top CEOs in Canada found that 'shareholder activism and unpredictable questions top the list of 'worst nightmares' at annual meetings.'[241]

On 20 May 1998 the U.S. Securities & Exchange Commission (SEC) decided that companies should not be allowed to exclude all shareholder resolutions raising workplace issues and matters of significant social policy. This reversed a 1992 SEC ruling (the Cracker Barrel case) that allowed companies to exclude such resolutions. The 1998 decision was a victory for social and environmental organisations and concerned shareholders, who had joined in an intense lobbying campaign aimed at getting the SEC to reverse its restrictive 1992 ruling.[242]

The Interfaith Center on Corporate Responsibility (ICCR) regularly publishes information about shareholder resolutions related to social responsibility.[243] A recent ICCR publi-

cation profiled 224 shareholder resolutions to 151 companies in 1999.[244] A number of these resolutions related to human rights issues, for example the following resolutions concern human rights in China:

i)   **Boeing**: The resolution asks Boeing to adopt 'basic human rights criteria for its business operation in and/or with the People's Republic of China' and to describe how it intends to implement them.

ii) **Exxon**: The resolution asks Exxon, in relation to an exploration venture in China, to review its 'code of business conduct with the view to including in it an explicit commitment to human rights, social justice and environmental responsibility' towards the communities in which the company operates.

iii) **General Motors and Lucent Technology**: Resolutions ask each company to adopt 'policies for all dealings with China,' including that it will not accept goods or services produced by slave or forced labour, not sell to any facility using slave or forced labour, and will pursue the right to on-site inspections to determine the existence of slave or forced labour.

iv) **Morgan Stanley**: The resolution refers to Morgan Stanley having underwritten bonds for China's State Development Bank, which loaned funds for the controversial Three Gorges dam. The resolution asks Morgan Stanley to report on its underwriting, investing and lending criteria, 'with the view to incorporating criteria related to a transaction's impact on the environment, human rights and risk to the company's reputation.'[245]

The Washington, D.C.-based Investor Responsibility Research Center (IRRC) includes a Social Issues Service that 'offers impartial research and analysis on corporate social responsibility issues, particularly those raised in proxy statements and at corporate annual meetings.'[246] IRRC's Social Issues Service often addresses international human rights issues. For example, among its 1996 publications were in-depth background reports on 'Human Rights and Labor Rights Issues,'[247] 'International Business and Human Rights in

Nigeria,'[248] 'U.S. Business and Labor Rights in China,'[249] and 'U.S. Business in Burma (Myanmar).'[250] IRRC also publishes a monthly newsletter entitled *Corporate Social Issues Reporter.*[251]

A new internet site, 'The Shareholder Activism Center' (www.socialfunds.com), allows investors to tell companies their views on social issues (including human rights issues) when they arise in shareholder resolutions. Using the site, anyone (whether or not a shareholder) can send their views to an individual company or to a group of companies linked by issues. The messages do not constitute actual shareholder votes. The site was developed by the Interfaith Center on Corporate Responsibility.[252]

2.12 Socially-responsible investment

In November 1997 the Social Investment Forum estimated that $1.185 trillion was invested in the U.S. in managed portfolios using at least one social investment strategy; that was a 30-fold increase from 1984, and represented nearly one in ten dollars under professional management in the U.S. in 1997.[253] The number of U.S. mutual funds using social screens grew from four in 1984, to 45 in 1995, to 144 in 1997.[254]

The President of Calvert Group, which operates socially responsible funds in the U.S., commented in a 1984 article:

SRI [socially responsible investing] funds with stringent criteria in the area of human rights actively seek out companies that are making serious efforts to promote human rights at home and abroad. This may take the form of developing policies and programmes that follow higher standards than those required in host countries or adopting explicit human rights principles to guide their international operations....As the world moves ever closer to becoming a truly integrated global economy, human rights and the other key aspects of the behaviour of companies are likely to take on increased importance for more and more investors who will demand just as much emphasis on people as on profits.[255]

In the U.K. at the end of 1998 there were reportedly about 40 funds invested according to ethical criteria, with new launches almost monthly. The total invested in those funds was approximately £2 billion, four times the amount invested five years earlier.[256]

Organisations that provide social screening information to funds and investors are increasingly including human rights as one of the factors in their assessment of a company's record. Most of these screening agencies are based in North America and Europe, and unfortunately they often have difficulty obtaining information (positive or negative) about the details of a multinational company's human rights record (and social record generally) in its operations outside North America and Western Europe.

Therefore it is encouraging that in other parts of the world there are investment funds and screening organisations being established that monitor the social record of companies operating in their geographical area. For example, in 1992 the Community Growth Fund (CGF) was launched in South Africa as an investment fund for the retirement funds of seven black trade unions, with a set of 17 social criteria to determine its investments.[257] The criteria, revised over the years, include 'good conditions of employment,' 'commitment to development,' 'community participation and support,' and 'social impact.'[258] The Labour Research Service, based in Cape Town, conducts social screening of companies for the CGF.[259] Companies that did not meet the CGF's social criteria have reportedly taken steps to improve their record. A 1995 article noted: 'It is not financial clout that makes acceptance or rejection by the Community Growth Fund a critical issue. It is the signal which acceptance or rejection sends out – not only to the company's labour force and the broader labour movement but also to an increasingly perceptive section of the business community. Rejection by the fund...is a tip-off that while the financials may look impressive, all is not well on the operational front, specifically with regard to industrial relations.'[260]

By 1998 at least 13 other socially responsible investment funds reportedly had been launched in South Africa. These funds tend to focus their portfolios on the general upliftment of previously disadvantaged communities through infrastructure development in under-serviced areas, job creation, and economic enablement. A survey by the firm Alexander Forbes found that these investment funds have generated good returns for the investor.[261]

2.13 Monitors take advantage of the communications revolution

The Environmental Defence Fund's website (www.scorecard.org) is packed full of scientific information about the pollution record of individual corporations, ranked by industry and by type of pollution. It allows anybody in the U.S. to type in their postal code and get a list of the top ten polluters in their neighbourhood. Click on one of those polluters and you get a draft letter that you can edit asking the company why it has failed to improve its environmental performance. The site also provides a list ranking the environmental record of states, so U.S. citizens can write to their governor calling attention to areas where the state government has fallen short. A recent article in *The Economist* sees this website as an example of a democratisation of information, creating a new balance of power where the citizen no longer is in a position of weakness when challenging business and government on environmental and social issues:

An old lop-sidedness in democracy – big business and big government are better informed than individuals, so win most of the big arguments – is suddenly corrected. It used to be that executives and bureaucrats could assure small-fry citizens that problems had been analysed, scientists consulted, safeguards put into place. Now citizens no longer need to accept those assurances helplessly. They can log on to the Internet and check them, with a few clicks of a mouse.[262]

Human rights and development organisations may not be able to duplicate the features of the Environmental Defence Fund's website; social issues cannot be quantified and ranked in the same way as pollution levels. Nevertheless, they are also taking advantage of the communications revolution. They are using the internet to gather and publicise information about the social record of companies worldwide. Pierre Sané, Secretary General of Amnesty International, noted recently: 'The fact is that human rights groups are now so numerous that it makes it much more difficult to suppress information, especially in the age of the Internet.'[263]

2.14 A need for more attention to the private sector's responsibility to promote human rights

Much of the focus of those monitoring business and human rights has been on alleged acts of irresponsibility, often by companies in the oil, mining or apparel industries. The scrutiny of these companies and any others allegedly contributing to human rights violations needs to be continued, indeed heightened. Acts of irresponsibility by business should always be a top priority for human rights monitors.

But human rights and development advocates, and the business community itself, also need to give increased attention to articulating and monitoring the positive responsibilities of all companies to promote human rights and sustainable development. This is particularly important now because a new league of multinational companies, the 'knowledge-based companies,'[264] are becoming larger and more powerful. Their work focuses on technology, computer networks, software, semiconductors, telecommunications, the internet and biotechnology. Their names include Microsoft, Intel, Cisco, Lucent, AOL, Yahoo and Amgen.

If anyone doubts the astounding growth and economic power of these companies, the market capitalisation (commonly referred to as 'market cap': the total market value of all outstanding shares, computed by multiplying the number of shares times the market price) of Microsoft on 10 April 1999 ($475.7 billion) was larger than the market cap of all the following oil companies put together (all figures reflect 10 April 1999)[265]: Exxon ($181.6 billion), Mobil ($73.4 billion), Chevron ($61.4 billion), Texaco ($31.0 billion), Total ($29.8 billion), Atlantic Richfield ($25.1 billion), Enron ($21.2 billion), CONOCO ($15.0 billion), Phillips Petroleum ($12.2 billion), Unocal ($8.8 billion), and Occidental Petroleum ($6.4 billion). If Exxon and Mobil are deleted from that list, Intel ($217.5 billion) had a market cap greater than the other nine oil companies combined. Cisco ($188.7 billion), Lucent ($168.2 billion) and America Online ($163.7) each had a greater market cap than eight of those oil companies put together (excluding Exxon, Mobil and Chevron). Even Yahoo ($41.5 billion) had a market cap almost equal to four oil companies combined: CONOCO, Phillips, Unocal, and Occidental. On 22 April 1999 the market capitalisation of Royal Dutch/Shell was $187 billion; BP Amoco was $171.2 billion.[266] In December 1997 the market cap of General Electric was roughly $241 billion, then greater than the combined value of the stock markets of Malaysia, Indonesia, Thailand, the Philippines and Korea.[267] Today Microsoft's market cap is larger than that of General Electric. There are many more technology companies than oil companies or apparel companies, they are growing at a much faster rate, and most of them are already international players.

The new technology companies are much less likely than some traditional companies to be displacing people, having contacts with a country's security forces, causing major environmental damage, operating sweatshops, using forced labour or using child labour. Their success is not based primarily on extracting resources from the earth or physical labour from people; it is based mainly on mobilising knowledge from the brains of their employees and utilising skills of a highly-trained workforce. As Peter Drucker says:

The industries that have moved into the center of the economy in the last forty years have as their business the production and distribution of knowledge and information, rather than the production and distribution of things. The actual product of the pharmaceutical industry is knowledge; pill and prescription are no more than packaging the knowledge.[268]

An April 1999 *International Herald Tribune* article drew attention to this focus on knowledge: 'With cash, stock options and the promise of vast resources, Microsoft Corp. is luring faculty elites to its research center at a pace so fast that some campus departments say they are being picked clean.'[269]

What responsibilities do these huge technology companies have to use their tremendous resources, skills and influence to contribute positively to the societies that supply them with markets, workers and customers? How should they be contributing to sustainable development and to civil society? What role should they play in improving education, reducing poverty, protecting the environment, and promoting human rights and the rule of law?

The human rights guidelines for companies articulated by human rights organisations, development agencies, business people and others (referred to elsewhere in this report) help to answer these questions. But more work needs to be done by human rights and development advocates to explain the positive responsibilities of business, to challenge companies to act, and to engage directly with the 'knowledge companies' that so far have tended to be on the sidelines of human rights debates.

3. Steps towards change

What are business membership organisations saying about human rights? ■ What kind of human rights policies and principles have companies been adopting? ■ What sort of human rights training should a company provide its employees? ■ What is the significance of external monitoring of a company's human rights practices?

3.1 Business groups putting human rights on their agenda

'The Caux Round Table Principles for Business,' adopted by a group of U.S., Japanese and European business leaders in 1994, state that business has certain responsibilities, including the following:

We believe that as global corporate citizens, we can contribute to such forces of reform and human rights as are at work in the communities in which we operate. We therefore have a responsibility in those communities to…respect human rights and democratic institutions, and promote them wherever practicable.[270]

In 1997, 14 Canadian companies announced an 'International Code of Ethics for Canadian Business.'[271] The code says: 'We believe that wealth maximization for all stakeholders will be enhanced by resolution of outstanding human rights and social justice issues.' Signatory companies pledge that they will 'support and promote the protection of international human rights within our sphere of influence' and will 'not be complicit in human rights abuses.' Another section of the code says companies will 'strive for social justice and promote freedom of association and expression in the workplace' and will 'ensure consistency with universally accepted labour standards, including those related to exploitation of child labour.'[272]

In April 1998 the Confederation of Danish Industry published *Industry and Human Rights*, a guide to help companies come to grips with human rights issues. This guide was developed in co-operation with the Danish Center for Human Rights.[273] The introduction states that the guide is intended for use by companies operating in or trading with countries being criticised for human rights violations. 'Its sole aim is to help companies recognise that they share a common responsibility, which society is increasingly imposing upon them, for the protection of human rights.'[274]

In the U.S., Business for Social Responsibility (BSR) is an alliance of over 1400 member companies and affiliated companies.[275] Its Business and Human Rights Program helps companies:

i) develop company human rights policies and systems for independent monitoring;

ii) engage in dialogue with human rights organisations, labour unions and governments; and

iii) address issues arising through sourcing and manufacturing in developing countries, such as worker health and safety, child labour, forced labour, working conditions, and environmental standards.[276]

The BSR website provides extensive information about human rights designed to help companies develop their policies and practices.[277]

The Confederation of Norwegian Business and Industry (NHO) has published a detailed checklist on human rights issues for companies, entitled 'Human rights from the perspective of business and industry – a checklist.'[278] The checklist, available in English and Norwegian, was drafted in cooperation with Amnesty International. It includes passages from relevant articles of the Universal Declaration of Human Rights, followed by questions companies should ask themselves when formulating their policies. The NHO notes that the Norwegian Government is 'calling for companies to take a more conscious, responsible position on human rights': 'Respecting and promoting human rights is an integral part of Norway's foreign and development co-operation policies. Accordingly, government assistance to Norwegian businesses abroad is based on the assumption that business and industry are willing to undertake this responsibility.'[279] The NHO says 'it is in companies' own best interests to foster respect for the principles of constitutional justice and human rights':

The Norwegian authorities and public opinion within the country are becoming increasingly critical of businesses that try to ignore or avoid dealing with issues related to human rights. The respect accorded to enterprises is increasingly becoming a factor of whether and, if so, how they deal with such issues.[280]

The NHO notes that a company's human rights policy may include:

i) 'open support for the UN Universal Declaration on Human Rights and the ILO standards';

ii) 'measures that help raise awareness about internationally recognised human rights standards, including support for educational projects related to human rights'; and

iii) 'contact and dialogue with individuals, NGOs, other companies and local and national authorities on the question of how human rights can be protected and violations prevented.'[281]

The NHO says 'companies may also choose to establish a dialogue with the authorities on issues involving specific violations on the part of the authorities,' including raising cases of 'victims of torture, random arrests, illegal imprisonment or miscarriages of justice.'[282]

These initiatives provide important recognition by the business community that support for, and promotion of, human rights are not outside the scope of the private sector's responsibilities. As for the voluntary codes, they are significant but not sufficient. Maurice Williams, President of the Society for International Development, has drawn attention to the fact that private sector codes are no substitute for enforced standards of public policy:

While these declarations of intentions are praiseworthy, they are entirely voluntary and hortatory. Systematic reporting on their application is largely lacking. Most private firms place the efficiency of their operations well to the fore of social concerns, as is the accepted business ethos. In fact, competition in the market-place is such that few firms are likely to take human rights standards seriously outside the framework of enforced public policy in favour of uniform application of social and environmental standards. Public spirited firms seek to cooperate with governments in the setting of such standards.[283]

3.2 Companies adopting human rights principles

Amnesty International's guidelines state that companies should adopt policies on human rights that:

i) explicitly support the Universal Declaration of Human Rights;

ii) set forth procedures to ensure all operations are examined for their potential impact on human rights;

iii) provide safeguards to ensure that company staff are never complicit in human rights abuses;

iv) enable issues about human rights and the rule of law to be raised with government authorities;

v) provide for human rights training of all employees within the company;

vi) commit the company to promote respect for international human rights.[284]

The International Confederation of Free Trade Unions (ICFTU, an independent organisation representing 125 million workers in 213 trade unions from 143 countries and territories) and International Trade Secretariats (ITS, the international trade unions for various employee sectors, associated with ICFTU) adopted in 1997 a 'Basic Code of Conduct covering Labour Practices,' a minimum list of standards that they consider should be included in all company codes of conduct covering labour practices.[285] The Basic Code focuses on internationally-recognised labour rights and refers to relevant ILO Conventions. Provisions of the ICFTU/ITS Basic Code include: freedom of association and the right to collective bargaining are respected; employment is freely chosen; there is no discrimination in employment; child labour is not used; living wages are paid; hours of work are not excessive; working conditions are decent; and the employment relationship is established. The ICFTU and ITS are discussing with a number of individual companies and industry associations the contents of labour practice codes and how those codes will be implemented and monitored.[286]

Canadian law professor Craig Forcese set forth the following criteria for company policies on human rights in a publication of the Montréal-based International Centre for Human Rights and Democratic Development:

Businesses should introduce human rights codes of conduct and abide by country guidelines. Specifically, these codes and guidelines should contain:

■ *a pledge to observe the core labour rights, namely, freedom of association and the rights to organize and bargain collectively, a ban on convict and forced labour, non-discrimination in employment and a ban on exploitative child labour;*

■ *a pledge to observe other important labour rights; namely, safe and healthy working environments, fair wages, and fair working hours and overtime;*

■ *a pledge not to reinforce the repressive capacity of a repressive regime by generating products, revenue, infrastructure or lending credibility to the regime, with a repressive regime defined as one that is a systematic violator of human rights;*

■ *a pledge not to invest in countries in which the business's activities induce repressive activity or support the repressive capacity of a repressive regime or where the business cannot, by reason of the overall human rights envi-*

ronment, maintain the workplace standards set out in its code of conduct;

■ *a pledge to exert a positive effect by intervening with authorities and business partners to improve respect for fundamental human rights norms wherever the business is in a position to exert positive influence; and*

■ *mechanisms for independent monitoring, a guaranteed non-retaliation for workers reporting code violations and some provision for training employees and contractors to implement the code appropriately.[287]*

Human Rights Watch in 1996 identified five essential reasons why companies should have codes of conduct on human rights (and independent monitoring of their human rights practices):

1. *It is the right thing to do in terms of community responsibility;*

2. *Employees are more likely to identify with the goals of an organisation that respects human rights;*

3. *Consumers are increasingly well informed about how products are manufactured;*

4. *Local communities are demanding respect for human rights even if their governments do not;*

5. *Protection of corporate image by not being associated with human rights violations.[288]*

The changes in business thinking discussed in section 1, and the various pressures on the private sector discussed in section 2, have spurred some companies to adopt human rights policies. They do so partly as a defensive move: they want to avoid the media attention and reputation damage that Shell, Unocal, Nike, Rio Tinto, Freeport-McMoRan, Enron, BP and others have suffered in human rights controversies, or at least to be better prepared than those companies were. They also act to gain competitive advantage: they realise they will have to address human rights issues sooner or later, and doing it sooner will give them an advantage over corporations that lag behind; in recent decades they saw those companies that resisted environmental accountability (in the futile hope that interest would fade) suffer financially and in terms of reputation. Companies are starting to realise that in the next century it will be very difficult to be a world-class company if they have a second-class human rights record.

Until the late 1990s only a few companies had adopted policies that seriously addressed international human rights issues. Those in the forefront included Levi Strauss, Reebok and The Body Shop.

The Levi Strauss 'Global Sourcing & Operating Guidelines,' adopted in 1991, say that the company will only do business with partners that adopt certain employment, health and safety standards. Levi Strauss says that if it determines any business partner is in violation of these standards, 'the company may withdraw production from that factory or require that a contractor implement a corrective action plan within a specified time period. If a contractor fails to meet the corrective action plan commitment, Levi Strauss & Co. will terminate the business relationship.'[289] The guidelines also include the following provision: 'We will favor business partners who share our commitment to contribute to improving community conditions.'[290] The Levi Strauss 'Country Assessment Guidelines' say: 'The diverse cultural, social, political and economic circumstances of the various countries where Levi Strauss & Co. has existing or future business interests raise issues that could subject our corporate reputation and therefore, our business success, to potential harm. The Country Assessment Guidelines are intended to help us assess these issues.'[291] The guidelines say one of the factors the company assesses is 'whether the…[h]uman rights environment would prevent us from conducting business activities in a manner that is consistent with the Global Sourcing Guidelines and other company policies.'[292] Levi Strauss, applying its Country Assessment Guidelines, decided to withdraw operations from Burma (Myanmar) in 1992, stating: 'Under current circumstances, it is not possible to do business in Myanmar without directly supporting the military govern-

ment and its pervasive violations of human rights.'[293]

Reebok's 'Human Rights Production Standards,' adopted in 1992, say that the company's 'devotion to human rights worldwide is a hallmark of our corporate culture.'[294] The standards cover non-discrimination, working hours/overtime, forced or compulsory labour, wages, child labour, freedom of association, and workplace safety/health. Reebok says it applies these standards in its selection of business partners: 'To assure proper implementation of this policy, Reebok will seek business partners that allow Reebok full knowledge of the production facilities used and will undertake affirmative measures, such as on-site inspection of production facilities, to implement and monitor those standards.'[295] Reebok annually recognises four young human rights advocates with its Reebok Human Rights Award (a grant of $25,000 to a human rights organisation designated by each recipient).[296]

The Body Shop's 'Trading Charter,' adopted in 1994, includes the following statements:

We aim to ensure that human and civil rights, as set out in the Universal Declaration of Human Rights, are respected throughout our business activities. We will establish a framework based on this declaration to include criteria for workers' rights embracing a safe, healthy working environment, fair wages, no discrimination on the basis of race, creed, gender or sexual orientation, or physical coercion of any kind. We will support long term, sustainable relationships with communities in need. We will pay special attention to those minority groups, women and disadvantaged peoples who are socially and economically marginalised….We will institute appropriate monitoring, auditing and disclosure mechanisms to ensure our accountability and demonstrate our compliance with these principles.[297]

The Body Shop also has adopted a 'Statement of Human Rights Principles,' which includes the following assertions:

While we respect cultural differences, and are aware of the economic disparities that exist within and between countries, we believe that the civil, political, economic, social and cultural rights outlined in the Universal Declaration of Human Rights (UDHR) are

*universal, indivisible, interdependent and inter-relat-
ed. Our goal is to encourage the creation of working
and living conditions where people can fulfil their
potential, where their human rights are respected
without prejudice, and where they can determine their
own destiny. We will seek business partners who share
this commitment.*[298]

The Body Shop's principles include one of the
strongest statements of any company about its
responsibility to promote human rights in the
societies where it operates:

*Raising awareness of human rights at every level will
empower individuals and communities. We aim to
educate ourselves on human rights issues and to use
our influence and our trading relationships to promote respect for human rights. We will campaign passionately for human rights where we believe our
involvement will contribute to positive change.*[299]

The Body Shop has conducted through its
retail shops a number of campaigns on human
rights issues. For example, in 1998 The Body
Shop and Amnesty International joined forces
to celebrate the 50th anniversary of the
Universal Declaration of Human Rights with a
campaign that involved Body Shop customers
in over 1400 stores internationally 'making
their mark' (putting their thumbprint) on a
petition on behalf of human rights defenders;
over 3 million thumbprints reportedly were col-
lected.[300]

Today many more companies, including
Royal Dutch/Shell, BP Amoco, Nokia, Statoil,
Norsk Hydro, Rio Tinto, and BT (British
Telecommunications PLC), have adopted
human rights policies. The policies of several of
these companies explicitly state that the company supports the Universal Declaration of
Human Rights. For example, BP in 1998 incor-
porated the following statement into its business policies:

*We will pursue our business with integrity, respecting
the different cultures and the dignity and rights of
individuals in all the countries in which we operate.
We support the principles set forth in the UN
Universal Declaration of Human Rights, recognising
the role and enforcement responsibilities of governments.*[301]

BP noted in its 1987 social report that under its
self-certification process, each year about
10,000 employees in positions of responsibility
worldwide must certify that they understand the
business policies, that they have brought the
policies to the attention of their staff and any
third parties acting on BP's behalf, and that
they are to the best of their knowledge in compliance with the policies. They are instructed to
bring forward any concerns they might have
about implementation of the policies.[302]

Another example of a recently-adopted
human rights policy is that of Royal
Dutch/Shell. Its 'Statement of General
Business Principles' now includes provisions
recognising the responsibility of Shell companies:

To respect the human rights of their employees;....

*To conduct business as responsible corporate members
of society, to observe the laws of the countries in which
they operate, to express support for fundamental
human rights in line with the legitimate role of business and to give proper regard to health, safety and
the environment consistent with their commitment to
contribute to sustainable development.*[303]

In 1998 Shell published its first social report,
entitled *Profits and Principles – does there have to be
a choice?*[304] The introduction speaks of a thorough and far-reaching review Shell has been
carrying out, and says: 'We had looked in the
mirror and we neither recognised nor liked
some of what we saw.'[305] Shell says it is developing new thinking and processes to help it better
manage its social and ethical responsibilities, to
measure performance and to report regularly.
The report says the company supports the
Universal Declaration of Human Rights, and
has taken steps including the following 'to
ensure we act in the best possible way when confronted with human rights issues':

■ *We speak out in defence of human rights
  when we feel it is justified to do.*

■ *We engage in discussion on human rights
  issues when making business decisions.*

■ *We have established a regular dialogue with groups which defend human rights.*

■ *We are developing awareness training and management procedures to help resolve human rights dilemmas when they arise. This includes a guide to human rights for managers....*[306]

Shell's second social report, published in 1999, includes a progress report on the company's human rights commitments.[307] It explains that Shell's letter of assurance process (each of Shell's Country Chairmen is required to write an annual letter to the Group Managing Director explaining how the company's General Business Principles are being applied) now includes specific references to human rights. The report includes an explanation of Shell's policy on the use of force and firearms by security personnel.[308] It mentions that the company launched a special human rights site on its intranet (internal computer network). The section updating human rights developments in Nigeria includes the following statement: '[Shell] does not use force or seek armed intervention to suppress demonstrations by communities protesting peacefully, even if it disrupts production....It believes strongly that dialogue is the answer to such situations.'[309]

BT's board of directors reportedly approved a new statement of business practices in March 1999 that includes a section on human rights. Amnesty International's UK Business Group commented: 'This is a significant step for a company which has not been targeted by NGOs and therefore does not have a pressing need to improve its image and appease its critics.'[310] Jan Walsh, BT's Head of Corporate Reputation and Social Policy, said:

Our commitment to addressing the human rights context of our operations reflects our aspirations as a global company to minimise the risk of transgressing international law and of violating widely held norms of acceptable behaviour. The Universal Declaration of Human Rights is an appropriate framework for us to use because of its international legitimacy and because it will facilitate our future efforts to develop human rights benchmarks....[311]

Human rights and development advocates are watching to see how each new policy will be implemented and monitored, recognising that if a company adopts policies without also training staff, introducing accountability and providing for independent monitoring, there may be little change in corporate culture and conduct. What ultimately matters is what a company does in practice about human rights, not what it declares in its company code.

Looking at corporate codes referring to human rights issues that have been adopted so far, shortcomings are evident:

i)   Most human rights policies have been adopted by companies only after they and/or their industry have come under attack in connection with human rights abuses. Most codes with a human rights component are found at apparel companies and oil companies. It is very disappointing that companies in other industries are usually silent on the subject.

ii)   Of those corporate codes that do include mention of human rights issues, most take a minimalist approach, referring only to issues for which their industry has been criticised. For example, the codes of many apparel companies have provisions about working conditions and child labour/forced labour. While those commitments are welcome, there is seldom any reference at all to the company's responsibility to support and promote fundamental human rights in the wider society where it operates...indeed in apparel codes there is seldom any mention of the term 'human rights' at all.

iii) Some companies that adopt a code as a defensive measure in response to pressure do not give priority to implementing their code after the pressure abates. The Canadian Government drew attention to this problem in a 1998 Industry Canada report:

[W]hile codes are voluntary – firms are not legislatively required to develop or adhere to them – the term 'voluntary' is something of a misnomer. Voluntary codes are usually a response to the real or perceived threat of a new law, regulation or trade sanctions, competitive pressures or opportunities, or consumer

and other market or public pressures...[O]nce the code is in place, the initial pressure that led to its creation may dissipate, which could cause compliance among adherents to taper off.[312]

3.3 Human rights training for employees

Amnesty International states that companies can improve their ability to promote human rights by 'providing effective training for their managers and their staff in international human rights standards, preferably with input and assistance from non-governmental organizations.'[313] 'To be effective, a corporate human rights policy must become an integral part of the company's culture.'[314]

Too many companies that have adopted fine-sounding human rights principles have made little or no effort to train their managers and staff in the practical application of those policies, and have no system for assessing whether those principles are being implemented. In fact often employees are not even aware of such policies. When I have telephoned multinational companies that have adopted human rights principles to obtain a copy of the document that includes the policy, I have found that many employees are not even aware that such principles exist.

A recent report by the ILO about codes of conduct noted:

Not infrequently, codes launched with much publicity in an import country are unknown, unavailable or untranslated at producing facilities; even where available, workers may have no way of reading the code or reporting non-compliance without disciplinary treatment or dismissal....Experience suggests that the current lack of standardized principles and procedures hinders good quality in implementation of codes, and prevents the reporting of comparable data to help measure progress in the enterprise, and within or across industry sectors. The lack of standardization also contributes to suspicions of third parties about internal monitoring processes and exploitation of labour conditions due to cultural relativity in MNE [multinational enterprise] practices.[315]

Royal Dutch/Shell is one company that has taken some first steps in developing a training

process. Shell's training guide for managers, 'Business and Human Rights: A Management Primer,'[316] was written with the help of independent experts. Its foreword notes:

Western investments in developing countries, in particular, are increasingly the focus of human rights concerns. The power of 20th-century communications means that these debates, and the issues and experiences they spring from, can no longer remain internal to either our organisation, or anyone else's. They are public, and important to millions of people....We need to participate in this discussion with the care and thoughtfulness our companies have always brought to bear on important questions.[317]

The foreword goes on to say that the handbook was prepared 'to facilitate a better understanding of human rights, its history, vocabulary and dilemmas, and to help Shell companies identify and understand their role and responsibilities in supporting human rights.'[318]

One of the questions posed in the handbook is: 'How should a company be expected to express its support for international human rights standards in countries that don't fully observe them?'[319] The handbook admits that Shell needs to undertake more discussion of this dilemma, but notes it is vital for all employees to be aware of the company's societal responsibility 'to express support for fundamental human rights in line with the legitimate role of business.'[320] It goes on to say that Shell companies...

can develop human rights goals appropriate to their own situations, and commit to entering into dialogue with policymakers about the need to remove constraints on their ability to achieve them. How this dialogue is conducted – whether publicly or privately, for example – depends upon a company's assessment of the situation. While this may include an external communications strategy, the focus should remain on achievement of concrete human rights goals rather than 'playing to the gallery', either at home or abroad.[321]

Shell's 1999 social report refers to training of the company's security personnel:

In all countries where security personnel carry firearms they are trained in the responsible use of force. In addition, in 20 countries the armed security guards are trained in accordance with the latest (1st Jan 1998) Group Security guidelines on the use of force, which are based on UN principles and codes of conduct and on international human rights standards. Urgent efforts are in hand to ensure consistency with the latest Group guidelines in the remaining three countries.[322]

BP Amoco's steps to raise staff awareness about human rights have included developing intranet sites providing employees with specific guidance on human rights issues, and contact information for international human rights and development organisations.[323]

The Norwegian oil company Statoil, in its 1998 Annual Report, notes that it has started human rights training for its employees:

Respect for human rights will be demonstrated through Statoil's actions. The group faces social systems and attitudes in many of the countries in which it operates that do not accord with the values on which its business is based. In order to exert a positive influence, make its commercial principles known and participate in the dialogue on human rights in these nations, Statoil needs well-informed employees. An extensive internal training programme is building a foundation for translating the group's attitudes into practical action.[324]

It will be important for all companies to ensure that human rights training:

i)   explains in plain language international standards on civil, political, economic, social and cultural rights – and how those rights are relevant to the company's operations internationally and locally;

ii) includes among the trainers people from human rights NGOs and people who have practical experience addressing human rights issues in the particular country and locality;

iii) focuses not just on managers at headquarters, but is effectively delivered to all staff and managers at all the company's operations worldwide;

iv) is pragmatic and specific rather than academic and vague;

v)   addresses local issues and difficult fact situations that may arise in the particular country;

vi) is delivered in local languages whenever necessary to ensure full understanding by all staff;

vii) explains to employees how company procedures will ensure each staff member is individually accountable for applying the company's human rights policy, and how the overall policy will be implemented and independently monitored; and

viii) makes clear to employees how they can report non-compliance with the company's human rights principles without any risk of retaliation.

3.4 Independent monitoring

Amnesty International states:

All companies should establish mechanisms to monitor effectively all their operations' compliance with codes of conduct and international human rights standards. Such mechanisms must be credible and all reports must periodically be independently verifiable in a similar way to the auditing of accounts or the quality of products and services. Other stakeholders such as members of local communities in which the company operates and voluntary organizations should have an opportunity to contribute in order to ensure transparency and credibility.[325]

The Dutch Sections of Amnesty International and Pax Christi International note that a company should extend such a monitoring system to its suppliers, sub-contractors and joint ventures. They stress the importance of involving local organisations in the monitoring process:

Accuracy and credibility is enhanced if the monitoring programme involves local labour, human rights, religious or other institutions who have the trust of workers and knowledge of local conditions. Monitors rooted in local communities will be best qualified to detect essential, but not easily quantifiable, facts which relate to human rights, like non-discrimination, harassment, the right to organize, etc.[326]

Elaine Bernard, Executive Director of the Harvard Trade Union Program, has put forward 'general overall principles of independent monitoring' that she says are necessary 'to breathe life into the promise of any 'code of conduct' or indeed, any claims of 'good employer' practices':[327]

i) **Independent:** 'Monitoring must be independent of business and the government.'

ii) **Ongoing:** 'Monitoring must be ongoing, not ad hoc, nor simply a publicity, celebrity visit. Monitors must have ongoing access to both the workers and workplace – and workers must be able to talk with monitors in complete confidentiality and with no reprisals.'

iii) **Institutional:** 'Monitoring needs to be institutional and to have independent authority beyond a 'great man' or 'great woman'.' The monitoring agency needs sufficient resources.

iv) **Indigenous:** 'Monitoring must have an indigenous component. That is, it must be on the ground, with local people, who speak the language, who live in the country where workplaces are being monitored.'

v) **Trusted:** 'Monitoring groups must be trusted by the workers and with a track record within the country.'

vi) **Knowledgeable:** '[F]or monitoring to be truly effective, the monitors need to have people who have knowledge about the work process under review and an appreciation of what is common practice and what is not.'

vii) **Transparent:** 'The work of the monitoring group must be as open as possible. Transparency needs to be written into any monitoring agreement so that the monitors have the right to communicate information without corporate pre-screening or control.'[328]

Elaine Bernard says that if the above conditions cannot be met, NGOs 'should not be dragged into monitoring....For example, if rights are so consistently denied that there is no 'trusted' indigenous human rights or workers group to partner with, we should state openly that 'independent monitoring' is not possible in this environment – and furthermore, that any code of conduct under such circumstances is meaningless.'[329]

Richard Howitt, the Member of the European Parliament who introduced the recently-adopted European Parliament resolution concerning codes of conduct for European transnational corporations (described in section 2.4), has drawn attention to the need for independent monitoring:

I believe that voluntary codes of conduct on their own are inadequate. In the two years of preparation for this parliamentary report, I have observed that many companies and business associations express their codes in glossy documents with fine words. When I ask the question 'how are these to be implemented?', or 'how have these voluntary standards changed business practice?' or 'have they led to compensation for a complainant?', there is a deafening silence. This is not to say that these voluntary codes are drawn up in bad faith, which I don't believe to be the case. However, if these codes are to be worth the paper they are written on, companies and industry-wide associations who are responsible for them must place far greater emphasis on implementation, including independent monitoring, complaints mechanisms and redress. My resolution in the European Parliament was designed to encourage voluntary codes which are accompanied by such measures....No company can have a credible code of conduct, unless within that code is a system of monitoring and implementation.[330]

The U.S. Department of Labor, in a 1996 study of corporate codes dealing with child labour, noted that 'a credible system of monitoring – to verify that a code is indeed being followed in practice – is essential.' The study found that 'most of the codes...do not contain detailed provisions for monitoring and implementation,' 'many of the companies do not have a reliable monitoring system in place,' and where monitoring was undertaken 'there seems to be relatively little interaction between, on the one hand, monitors, and on the other hand, workers and the local community.' The study noted with concern: 'It also appears that monitors have a technical background in production and quality control and are relatively untrained with regard to implementation of labor standards.'[331]

Sir John Browne, BP Amoco's Chief Executive, recognised that social and human rights principles alone are not enough:

Setting and meeting one's own standards is only part of what is required. Companies need to win and retain public trust. That comes only through a track record of delivery and a transparency which allows everyone to see exactly what is happening. That means we have to be open to dialogue with local communities and non-governmental organisations and open to scrutiny even when it is uncomfortable. It also means we have to develop the means of verification, an independent auditing process to underpin the company's own assurance.[332]

BP's 1997 social report states: 'Assurances of good behaviour are insufficient without independent verification.'[333]

A recent *Economist* article noted: 'The best codes now tend to be monitored by outside auditors. Companies realise that merely making promises risks adding hypocrisy to the list of charges against them.'[334]

A leading book on the subject of corporate social auditing explains why there is increasing pressure on companies to have their human rights and social record independently assessed:

One common concern arises from the increased disclosure of corporate social and ethical performance; there is a need to establish methods for assessment, verification and disclosure that meet the requirements of both companies and outside parties. 'Glossy' social reporting no longer satisfies the demands of groups that have the power to support or undermine a company's market position, through organizing consumer boycotts or blocking planning permission. Nor does a gloss over a company's ethics help in attracting creative, dedicated and responsible employees who feel a strong sense of identity with the company and whose commitment is vital for overall business success. Shareholders themselves are also demanding to know more about social and ethical performance as an increasing number of high-profile cases highlight the financial consequences of unethical business behaviour.[335]

The New Economics Foundation, a London-based organisation which is working with companies to develop techniques for social auditing, emphasises that the integrity of a social audit is dependent on meaningful involvement of stakeholders in the process:

If the process is to be credible, then the dialogue with stakeholders must be meaningful and, most importantly, the key indicators which result from the accounting process must be developed by the stakeholders themselves, in line with international human rights instruments. So the paradox of how to measure human rights can perhaps be resolved if the assessment of the expression of rights involves the people affected.[336]

Few companies have commissioned an independent social audit, and even fewer have made them public. In India, The Tata Iron and Steel Company in 1979 was one of the first in the world to commission a social audit, carried out by a three-person committee (a judge and two professors). The audit was made public.[337]

The Body Shop in January 1996 published a statement of its social performance, that was independently verified by the New Economics Foundation. The Body Shop's auditing process involved participation by a committee of stakeholders. The company also commissioned Kirk Hanson, a professor of business ethics from Stanford University's Graduate School of Business, to evaluate the company's social record. The Body Shop's founders, Anita and Gordon Roddick, wrote about the social audit process in the company's *Social Statement 1995*:

We went into the social audit with a sense of 'damned if we do, damned if we don't'. We are pleased with the result. It has been a long and detailed process, which we now feel we can recommend to others. We are already finding that it is helping us run our business better and we are delighted to see that different parts of the business recognise the improvement points necessary to maintain the support of their stakeholders. We now have a list of strategic targets and priorities for action described as 'next steps' goals for each stakeholder group which will drive us on towards the millennium with greater confidence about those human relationships which are integral to our success.[338]

The Roddicks, publicly recognising both the positive and negative findings of Kirk Hanson's social evaluation, said: 'The integrity of the business shines through amidst some ineptitude, some lack of attention, some good old fashioned neglect....We have much to improve.'[339]

Kirk Hanson said of The Body Shop's social auditing process: 'To my knowledge, no other company has permitted such an extensive and public evaluation of its social record by an outside individual.'[340] He predicted that social auditing would become a more common practice: 'Social performance today has profound importance for commercial performance...the social audit will eventually be done much as the financial audit is now done.'[341]

In 1997 The Body Shop published its second Values Report, including a social audit independently verified by the New Economics Foundation.[342]

A precedent-setting 1996 independent monitoring agreement was the key to resolving a dispute that arose when a garment manufacturer in El Salvador supplying The Gap was accused of abuses including child labour, forced overtime, unsafe working conditions, and threats to prevent workers from organising.[343] The Gap had adopted a code of conduct before the allegations came to light, but according to the executive director of the U.S. National Labor Committee in Support of Democracy and Human Rights in El Salvador, no worker at the factory in El Salvador had ever seen the code, and it had not even been translated into Spanish.[344] The Gap and the Salvadorian supplier agreed to a system of periodic on-site visits to the factory by independent monitors. The Independent Monitoring Group is composed of the Human Rights Institute of the University of Central America, the Human Rights Office of the Archdiocese of San Salvador, and the Labour Studies Centre (CENTRA). Labour groups had insisted that independent monitoring was necessary to make The Gap's 'Sourcing Principles & Guidelines' work in practice. They believed that only independent monitors could ensure that the process would be thorough and objective, and ensure that workers would be able to speak freely without fear of harassment or loss of employment.[345]

The then U.S. Labor Secretary Robert Reich reportedly said The Gap's agreement was an 'important step' because the major retailers and manufacturers 'have been somewhat reluctant to police their contractors here and abroad.' He went on to say that 'this raises the question for other big retailers who haven't moved in this direction – why not?'[346]

U.S. President Clinton in 1996 appointed the Apparel Industry Partnership, a panel of representatives of apparel companies (including Liz Claiborne, Nike, Phillips Van-Heusen and Reebok) and non-governmental organisations (NGOs), to address the issue of sweatshops in the apparel industry. The task force's mandate was:

1. *To ensure that the products companies make and sell are manufactured under decent and humane working conditions, and*

2. *to develop options to inform consumers that the products that they buy are not produced under exploitative conditions.*[347]

The Apparel Industry Partnership released its 'preliminary agreement' in November 1998, including a 'Workplace Code of Conduct' and 'Principles of Monitoring,' to be administered by a new 'Fair Labor Association'; an 'amended agreement' was issued in June 1999.[348] The *New York Times* reported in November 1998: 'After the task force's 18 members remained stalemated for months, nine of the group's more centrist members began negotiating among themselves and finished thrashing out an agreement.'[349] Several key organisations that had been part of the Partnership (the Interfaith Center on Corporate Responsibility [ICCR]; the AFL-CIO; the Retail, Wholesale and Department Store Union; and UNITE, the nation's leading apparel union) rejected the agreement and refused to endorse it on the grounds that it was not strong enough.[350]

The Apparel Industry Partnership's 'Workplace Code of Conduct'[351] includes prohibitions against forced labour and child labour, a maximum work week of 60 hours, and recognition of freedom of association and the right of all employees to 'be treated with respect and dignity.' On the issue of wages, the agreement provides: 'Employers shall pay employees, as a floor, at least the minimum wage required by local law or the prevailing industry wage, whichever is higher....' The agreement also calls for a Department of Labor study on existing wages in relevant countries and how they compare with the amount needed to meet workers' basic needs. Critics said the agreement should have guaranteed a living wage; Reverend David Schilling of ICCR said: 'A factory may be clean, well organized and monitored, but unless the workers are paid a sustainable living wage, it is still a sweatshop.'[352]

The 'Principles of Monitoring'[353] say that independent external monitors should conduct periodic announced and unannounced visits to factories, and that the monitors should consult regularly with human rights, labour, religious and other local institutions likely to have the trust of workers and knowledge of local conditions. Critics said this did not ensure effective independent monitoring because it would allow companies to use their own auditing firms to carry out the monitoring without requiring active participation by local human rights organisations that would be more likely to act independently and to have the trust of workers. UNITE said the agreement 'allows companies to pick the factories that will be inspected by monitors chosen and paid by the company'[354]; 'the companies pick their monitors and the factories to be monitored so there won't be surprise inspections.'[355] UNITE also expressed concern that...

this agreement will reinforce the tendency to view voluntary corporate codes of conduct as a substitute for the enforcement of existing laws and the adoption of legislation and trade agreements designed to protect the rights of workers in the global economy. While such codes can in some circumstances supplement the rule of law in protecting workers rights, they are a step backward when they undercut the demands and actions of the anti-sweatshop movement and allow corporations to carry on business as usual.[356]

The agreement was also criticised by UNITE and others on the grounds that it allowed companies to continue to produce goods in countries that systematically deny worker rights. Sister Dolores Brooks of ICCR said: 'We are pleased that the Workplace Code includes respect for the right of workers to freely associate and bargain collectively. However, the Agreement does not spell out what companies need to do in countries where this internationally-recognized right is denied.'[357]

The agreement calls for creation of a Fair Labor Association (FLA) to certify monitors and expel companies not in compliance.[358] Within three years of signing on, companies are required to have 30 % of factories monitored by external monitors; in subsequent years about 10 % of a company's factories must be inspected annually. Critics said 10% per year is not enough.[359]

Four NGO members of the Apparel Industry Partnership that supported the final agreement (Lawyers Committee for Human Rights, International Labor Rights Fund, Robert F. Kennedy Memorial Center for Human Rights, National Consumers League) said:

[While the accord] is not a perfect agreement, it does lay the foundation for creating a practical and enforceable monitoring system that will help improve working conditions....The FLA [Fair Labor Association] will accredit independent external monitors; oversee the monitoring process, including final decision-making as to which factories are subjected to independent monitoring; decide whether individual companies are in compliance with FLA standards, based on a review of reports by these monitors; and report publicly each year on the performance of each company that is participating in the process.[360]

As of 12 September 1999, ten companies had joined the FLA agreement: Adidas, Kathie Lee Gifford, Levi-Strauss, Liz Claiborne, LL Bean, Nicole Miller, Nike, Patagonia, Phillips Van-Heusen and Reebok.[361] On 9 September 1999 the FLA announced the appointment of Charles Ruff as the first chair of its Board of Directors.[362] Mr Ruff served as White House Counsel from 1997-1999; his previous positions include U.S. Attorney for the District of Colombia, Acting Deputy Attorney General in the Department of Justice, Director of the Watergate Special Prosecution Force, and Chair of the Multinational Panel to Inquire into the Curbing of Violence in the South African Elections. The FLA said on 9 September that it plans to hire its first executive director during the next month, that it would begin active operations later in 1999, and that the first inspections of factories would take place during the year 2000.[363]

Over 100 U.S. universities are affiliated with the FLA, in an effort to ensure that companies producing goods under their licenses are operating in accordance with the Association's principles.[364] But United Students Against Sweatshops (USAS) is calling on universities not to affiliate with the FLA, and instead to join their Worker Rights Consortium, a more rigorous monitoring system requiring that companies pay a living wage that meets the basic needs of workers, and publicly disclose the location of their factories so that human rights and labour groups can independently monitor them.[365] Jess Champagne, a member of the USAS Coordinating Committee and a Yale University student, reportedly stated in October 1999: 'We…want truly independent and effective verification by local groups who are trusted by workers to ensure that universities' codes of conduct are being enforced.'[366]

The University of Michigan reportedly will be adding the following statement to all its licensing agreements with apparel companies:

Effective not later than January 1, 2000, The University of Michigan will require each licensed manufacturer to disclose to the U of M the location (name, city and street address) of each factory used in the production of all items which bear The University of Michigan marks. The University of Michigan reserves the right to disclose this information to third parties, without restriction as to its further distribution in conjunction with The University of Michigan Advisory Committee on Labor Standards and Human Rights.[367]

In October 1999, Nike became the first large apparel company to disclose the names and locations of overseas factories which make athletic gear carrying the names of U.S. universities; the company listed the details of 42 factories in 11 countries on its website.[368] Several universities had threatened to terminate licenses with manufacturers that do not identify their factories; Nike's announcement was expected to put considerable pressure on other apparel makers to do the same. U.S. student groups and anti-sweatshop groups, which had been campaigning for such disclosure on the grounds that it is a prerequisite for allowing independent groups to check working conditions, welcomed Nike's move. Eric Brakken, an organiser for United Students Against Sweatshops (a

coalition of university groups), commented: 'What Nike did is important. It blows open the whole notion that other companies are putting forward that they can't make such disclosures.'[369]

In another initiative, five U.S. universities (members of the Collegiate Licensing Company) are undertaking a factory monitoring pilot programme in late 1999 with Verité,[370] an independent monitoring organisation based in Massachusetts. Under the programme independent monitors will visit factory sites where merchandise bearing the university logos are produced. The monitors will work with management and employees with the aim of ensuring compliance with labour code standards; a report will be prepared for each site detailing what steps were taken to comply with code standards. The objective of the pilot project is to develop case studies of code implementation and to demonstrate how an independent third party can assist manufacturers in resolving compliance issues.[371]

In August, September and October 1999 nine major U.S. retailers (Nordstrom, Gymboree, Cutter & Buck, J. Crew, Brylane L.P., DonnaKaran International, Phillips-Van Heusen, Polo Ralph Lauren and The Dress Barn) agreed to help fund an independent monitoring scheme for the factories they use in the Northern Marianas Islands (a U.S. commonwealth in the Pacific; Saipan is the largest island). The monitoring reportedly will be organised by Verité, and will include unannounced factory visits and investigation of complaints by workers.[372] The agreement was part of a settlement by those companies of a class action lawsuit brought against 18 retailers for allegedly conspiring with Marianas factory owners to deprive apparel workers of labor rights.[373] As of 7 October 1999, litigation in that case was still pending against other major U.S. retailers including The Gap, Tommy Hilfiger and Wal-Mart.[374]

On 18 October 1999 Reebok made public a detailed report by an independent Indonesian research firm which criticised working conditions at two Indonesian factories employing 10,000 workers producing Reebok footwear. The report, entitled *Peduli Hak*, is available on Reebok's website.[375] The report faults the factories on a number of counts, including: managers failed to communicate adequately with workers, most workers were functionally illiterate and could not understand their rights relating to overtime pay or the collective bargaining agreement, it was more difficult for women to obtain promotions, and health and safety procedures were deficient (especially concerning the use and handling of chemicals). The report mentions some corrective steps taken by managers at the two factories, but also indicates issues management has failed to address. Reebok said that based on the report it has pressed for improvements to the factories costing $500,000.[376] The two factories are not owned by Reebok, but they reportedly account for more than 75 percent of Reebok's footwear production in Indonesia. Reebok said it has made Indonesian-language copies of the report available to the factory workers, and presented the report at a meeting with its footwear contractors.[377] Reebok stated it is 'the first company in the footwear industry to make public an in-depth, third-party critique of labor conditions in factories making its product.'[378] The monitoring firm reportedly had full access to factory records and workers, and spent over 1400 hours inspecting the factories, observing working procedures and interviewing workers.[379] Reebok says it 'guaranteed that the research team would be able to work independently, without intervention from Reebok or the factory management.'[380] Reebok Chairman Paul Fireman said 'We have raised the ante with external monitoring, because we had gone as far as we could by ourselves.'[381] He also made the following comments:

Why did we undertake this potentially damaging workplace assessment, and why was it important to make the results public? The simple answer is because of the commitment we at Reebok have made to respect the fundamental human rights of the nearly 25,000 workers in Asia who produce our footwear....But there is another reason, which is just as important. We want to encourage other multinational corporations that may be reluctant to open the doors of the factories manufacturing their products to in-depth inspections. Quite simply, we want to show that a detailed, critical report about factory conditions can be disclosed without the sky falling. And we'd like to change the attitude that has prevailed among many companies for many years – that they do not have any real responsibility for conditions in factories they do not own, or for the treatment of workers who are not their employees.[382]

Reaction to Reebok's release of the *Peduli Hak* report was generally positive. Sidney Jones, Director of Human Rights Watch Asia, stated: 'If companies are going to think about truly independent studies of their overseas operations and taking real steps to improve the conditions of these workers, this is a useful example. They asked the right questions, developed a useful methodology, and they've done it all with the fullest possible transparency and made the findings public.'[383] Scott Greathead, CEO of World Monitors (a New York business and human rights consulting firm), said: 'There's a new corporate awareness that honesty and full disclosure are better than hiding behind veils of secrecy.'[384] While human rights advocates generally welcomed the initiative, some have observed that there are deeper issues which still need to be addressed, and they are calling on Reebok to provide better wages and to allow the workers to form unions. David Schilling of the Interfaith Center on Corporate Responsibility said: 'I would have hoped there would have been a greater examination on the right to freely associate in the workplace.'[385] Jeff Ballinger, a consultant at the John F. Kennedy School of Government at Harvard University and a member of Press for Change (which educates consumers on factory conditions in Asia), commented: 'This is the company that moved to China and Indonesia to get away from union contracts. They say that this is a communication problem. It's really a power distribution problem. These workers lack the power to represent themselves.'[386]

Shortly after Reebok's report was released, Aaron Bernstein (*Business Week* Associate Editor, respected for his coverage of global labour issues) reported that apparel company Liz Claiborne had given *Business Week* a copy of 'a remarkably candid outside report on a Guatemalan factory' which belongs to a Liz Claiborne supplier.[387] The report was prepared by the Commission for the Verification of Corporate Codes of Conduct (Coverco), formed in 1997 by Guatemalan religious and human rights activists. The report details a number of abuses, including 16-year-olds pressured to work overtime and complaints about inaccurate wage payments. Bernstein noted that it also 'tells how a line supervisor refused to allow a pregnant worker to leave for the hospital when she went into labor – implying that the delay may have led to her baby's being stillborn the next day.'[388] The report says that Coverco discussed the problems with plant managers, who addressed some problems but not others. Eventually the factory's owner replaced the managers, and Coverco says cooperation with managers has now improved. Roberta Karp, Liz Claiborne's General Counsel, said: 'This is exactly what we wanted: to learn what the problems were and figure out how to make them better.'[389]

Bernstein also reported in *Business Week* that Mattel, the toy company, was planning to publish in November 1999 a 'comprehensive review of eight plants in four countries [China, Indonesia, Malaysia and Thailand], using hundreds of specific labor standards.'[390] While the initiatives by Reebok and Liz Claiborne were one-off pilot projects, Mattel has appointed an outside group (Mattel Independent Monitoring Council for Global Manufacturing Principles) to develop and implement a monitoring system. The head of the Monitoring Council is S. Prakash Sethi, a management professor at Baruch College in New York with experience in monitoring codes of conduct. Mattel's standards for its factories are practical and precise, specifying for example how many toilets are required per worker and how many calories company cafeterias should serve workers each day. Sethi says that the Monitoring Council has 'tried to build criteria to measure objective outcomes, like square feet in a worker dorm, which hasn't been done before.'[391]

Referring to the initiatives by Reebok, Liz Claiborne and Mattel, Bernstein commented in *Business Week*: 'All three companies should be applauded for the breakthrough: The audits mark the first time companies have allowed truly independent outsiders with expertise in labor issues to rake over their factories – and then make the unpleasant findings public.' Bernstein observed that this 'new level of scruti-

ny' marks 'a turning point in the anti-sweatshop movement;' he believes 'other companies will have a more difficult time dragging their heels.'[392] He concluded:

The pioneers have shown that outside monitoring by human-rights groups can work, even if the results are painful or embarrassing. Other manufacturers or retailers, largely on the sidelines, should set aside their qualms and join their colleagues as they begin, little by little, to lift global labor standards.[393]

SA 8000 (Social Accountability 8000), the anti-sweatshop initiative by the Council on Economic Priorities (see section 2.6), aims to provide global standards on workers' rights and factory conditions, applicable internationally to all companies. SA 8000 includes a call for companies to pay a living wage. In 1997 CEP set up the Council on Economic Priorities Accreditation Agency (CEPAA), an association to administer SA 8000 and to accredit those who will serve as external monitors to assess compliance with the standards. CEPAA's international advisory board consists of representatives from business and NGOs, as well as academics.[394]

There is increasing pressure on companies to move towards 'social audits' that are accorded the same priority and conducted with the same rigour as financial audits. This does not mean that such audits should be the exclusive preserve of the same accounting firms that carry out financial audits.

Accounting firms and management consulting firms may be able to play a useful role in social audits, particularly in terms of ensuring that the process is correct and thorough, and that standards are applied uniformly. Auditing firms are showing interest in the market for social auditing. KPMG has created an ethical unit to provide what it describes as 'an innovative service to assist companies to develop and assess their performance in social and environmental management.'[395] Pricewaterhouse-Coopers (PWC) has launched a Corporate Accountability and Responsibility Evaluation Program that offers companies a computer software package to help them assess ethical performance.[396] James Warren, a partner in PWC's office in Guangzhou, China, said in

February 1999 that before late 1997 ethical audits were rare, but in 1998 PWC conducted 1500 inspections in Guangdong province alone, and the call for them is growing.[397] Dr Jennifer Woodward, a consultant on Global Risk Management Solutions for PWC, recently noted:

Increasingly we are seeing companies recognise that human rights are the business of business....[P]ublicly communicated policies [on human rights] are a good start. There is a need, however, to find ways of embedding these policies into corporate culture so that they are integrated into the day-to-day management of the business....Work on developing effectiveness indicators for human rights is at a very early stage. PricewaterhouseCoopers' Reputation Assurance framework (RA5) includes a blend of qualitative and quantitative indicators to assist a company to measure and benchmark the effectiveness of its response to human rights issues. We acknowledge that these performance indicators are far from definitive. Therefore we are working with Amnesty International and other human rights organisations to develop a more complete and rigorous set of human rights benchmarks. In general, as the shift towards globalisation continues, more and more business people will find themselves facing human rights issues. Gradually we will see a shift from managing reputation crises following a media exposé, to companies gaining positive competitive advantage for their good record on human rights.[398]

While traditional accounting and management consulting firms may be able to play an important, contributory role in social auditing, they do not have a level of expertise and experience in social issues that would enable them to be the primary assessor in the monitoring of human rights issues. Moreover they may not be perceived by the public, by workers and by local stakeholders as being sufficiently independent of the company concerned, particularly if they have an ongoing contractual relationship with the company. The Nike case, described elsewhere in this report, demonstrates the limitations of using a traditional auditing firm for social audits. When allegations of abuses in Nike's Asian factories first arose in 1996, Nike denied the allegations and said: 'Every Nike subcontractor is subject to systematic, unan-

nounced evaluation carried out by Ernst & Young.'[399] If that was indeed the case, the Ernst & Young oversight of labour issues apparently was not as effective as it should have been; it has since been recognised that there were a number of serious shortcomings at Nike's Asian factories in 1996. Human rights advocates who conducted a 1996 fact-finding mission examining Nike's factories in Indonesia concluded:

The Ernst & Young audits are thoroughly inadequate, mainly because the company is unknown to workers and hence not trusted. Workers are well aware that revealing the truth (let alone active dissent) often leads to reprisals....Through interviews with workers last week, the delegation discovered that the Ernst & Young monitoring teams are concerned primarily with product quality and whether production quotas are being met. Groups of workers at three separate factories were unanimous in claiming that monitors 'never ask questions about the workers or conditions in the factories.' At least two Nike-producing facilities weren't even audited in the last year.[400]

The Independent Monitoring Group of El Salvador (IMGES), established to monitor The Gap code of conduct in El Salvador as discussed above, argues that 'for monitoring to function properly, monitors must be trusted by the workers. And – given the harsh and bitter experience that many [workers] face – representatives of local, respected civil society organizations will always be more trusted than outside auditing firms.'[401]

An International Labour Office report recently noted: 'Some evidence indicates that traditional financial accounting firms may be less independent due to inexperience in the detection of workplace violations and pre-existing contractual relationships with enterprise management.'[402]

The Interfaith Center on Corporate Responsibility has been closely involved with monitoring issues, including the monitoring agreement for The Gap in El Salvador. The organisation says:

We believe local NGOs must play a central role in monitoring the workplace standards because local NGOs have skills that auditing, accounting and public relations firms do not....Monitors hired by compa-

nies to do social audits are trained to look at pages of figures, analyze [data] and check for quantifiable code violations. The skills required to detect violations of worker rights are different. Serious violations of freedom of association and various forms of harassment of workers often go undetected by auditors who come into an area, visit a plant, then leave. Independent monitors made up of local NGOs, rooted in local communities and having the trust of employees, are better qualified to detect the essential, but less quantifiable, elements in the workplace which relate to human respect, nondiscrimination, right to freely associate and to work in [a] safe environment free from fear.[403]

Many multinational companies that have recently adopted human rights principles have tended to be slow in adopting a system for independent monitoring or auditing. Some of them seem to be stalled at the point of discussing a range of alternative complex procedures for auditing and trying to decide how stakeholders should be consulted and who should be involved in carrying out the audit. While it is important to ensure an effective process for an independent social audit, there is a danger that companies may spend too much time discussing procedure at company headquarters and delay for too long the day when there is some practical focus on substance by genuinely independent monitors where it matters, at the site of their operations. Social auditing should not be looked upon as an all-or-nothing proposition. Even if a company decides it needs more time to finalise plans for a comprehensive independent social audit, that should not prevent some form of pragmatic independent human rights monitoring from going ahead in the meantime.

Many companies, even some of those that endorse the notion of independent monitoring, seem to be finding it difficult in practice to take the step of agreeing to have their operations inspected by genuinely independent monitors. This is not surprising; companies are accustomed to having total control over their operations, and to being very careful in how they project the company's image to the outside world. But attempts by company managers to control the monitoring process by assigning the task to an auditing firm or organisation that is

too closely associated with the company will be seen by many as more of a public relations exercise than a meaningful form of verification. Those with ultimate responsibility for monitoring must be knowledgeable about the local human rights situation, trusted by workers and stakeholders, and genuinely independent – not under the company's control or influence at all, and not in an ongoing business relationship with the company. There must be no grounds for any reasonable person to question the absolute impartiality of the monitors.

Some companies also resist independent monitoring and particularly the idea of publishing the results because they believe public criticism of the company is based on misperceptions, and they do not welcome the idea of engendering further public discussion of the company's perceived shortcomings. As Gordon and Anita Roddick commented when the 1995 independent social evaluation of The Body Shop was released:

One of the difficult lessons we have learned and perhaps are still learning is that although perception and our view of reality are often poles apart, it does not matter a damn. We must deal with perception as if it were reality, otherwise nothing changes. Our legendary grouchiness under criticism has sometimes stemmed from this perception/reality gap combined with a sense of unfairness, but we have promised to do better. This report has been a major step along the way.[404]

When The Body Shop commissioned and later published the independent audit, and when it accepted that along with the company's significant social achievements there were some shortcomings that needed attention, the public tended to welcome what it saw as signs of corporate humility, openness and integrity.

In this new era those companies that insist their social record is irreproachable and resist independent monitoring are inviting the very criticism they seek to avoid.

3.5 Companies working in partnership with the United Nations and World Bank

One recent example of companies addressing human rights and development issues is NetAid, launched on 8 September 1999. NetAid was formed by Cisco Systems (the world's leading supplier of computer networking hardware) and the U.N. Development Programme (UNDP). NetAid's website says it is 'the beginning of a new, long-term effort to utilize the unique networking capabilities of the Internet to promote development and alleviate extreme poverty across the world. The NetAid Foundation will serve as a global exchange point to link people to successful agents and agencies of change.'[405] NetAid states that its mission is to 'use the Internet as a medium of social and economic change' aimed at building 'a community of conscience dedicated to providing basic needs: food, shelter, legal protection, human rights and health care.'[406] Cisco's Executive Vice President, Don Listwin, said NetAid's goal is 'to provide a conduit for foundations, volunteer groups, corporations and individuals who have prospective solutions for Third World poverty to connect with people in poor countries who need help in obtaining education, finding markets for products, contacting health care providers or organizing workers.'[407] He said Cisco has a social conscience, but also recognises that as the internet grows worldwide, 'we'll be bringing more people into our business ecosystem.'[408] The UNDP plans to help people in less developed countries get computer access to NetAid through the development of local internet access centers.[409] NetAid's website provides suggestions on how people can take action on these issues, and includes sections on 'ending hunger,' helping refugees,' 'saving the environment,' 'securing human rights,' and 'relieving debt.'[410] Two other companies, KPMG (a leading accounting, tax and consulting firm) and Akamai Technologies (an internet communications company), have joined Cisco in sponsoring NetAid.[411] Cisco and KPMG reportedly have each agreed to spend up to $20 million on the project.[412] Televised rock concerts to be held on 9 October 1999 in New York, London and Geneva will help finance and publicise NetAid.[413] At the launching of NetAid, U.N. Secretary General Kofi Annan remarked: 'NetAid is an inspiring example of the kind of corporate citizenship and public-private partnership that will be crucial in addressing the challenges of the 21st century.'[414] John Chambers, President and CEO of Cisco Systems, said: 'Netaid.org enables ordinary citizens as well as world leaders and major artists to take action to fight extreme poverty around the world. The Internet already has made a difference in the way business is done around the world. Now the world's most powerful web site can help make the difference in eliminating one of the globe's most pressing problems.'[415]

Observers are watching to see how effective NetAid will be in making a difference at the grassroots level, and the extent to which it can overcome criticism that arose earlier in 1999 when the UNDP entered into another partnership with companies. Some NGOs criticised the UNDP for entering into a partnership with at least 16 multinational companies (including Dow Chemical, Rio Tinto, Citibank and AT&T) that paid $50,000 each towards establishing a 'Global Sustainable Development Facility' (GSDF).[416] The companies were reportedly told by the UNDP that they would 'benefit from the advice and support of UNDP through a special relationship.'[417] Critics said that some of the companies joining that partnership had 'tarnished records on human rights, labor and the environment,' and that the partnership offered these companies 'an opportunity to greenwash their images for cheap' while doing little to advance the UNDP's mission of serving the world's poor.[418] Ward Morehouse, president of the Council on International and Public Affairs, said: 'The U.N. should be monitoring the human rights and environmental impacts of corporations in developing and industrialized nations, not granting special favours.'[419] Joshua Karliner, Executive Director of the Transnational Resource and Action Center (TRAC), added: 'The needs of poor communities around the world constantly conflict with corporate goals. Corporations often use child labor, obstruct trade unions, and engage in practices that destroy natural resources and pollute poor communities.'[420] The UNDP defended the GSDF partnership, saying that '[t]he question...is not whether global corporations will increase their investments in developing countries, but how we can, as UNDP and others who are committed to sustainable human development, seek to ensure that at least some of these investments occur in ways that are pro-poor, pro-environment, pro-jobs and pro-women.'[421] The UNDP pledged to 'ensure that projects that would be coming under this initiative meet rigorous criteria, and are in compliance with all standards that the United Nations stands by.'[422]

The website of Corporate Watch (whose parent organisation is TRAC) includes a section entitled 'Corporatization of the United Nations.' Corporate Watch condemns the U.N.'s increasing links with multinational corporations, commenting that 'the UN seems to be scrambling for corporations' support, regardless of their social and environmental impact.' The website criticises various collaborations between the U.N. and corporations, including The Business Humanitarian Forum, co-chaired by the U.N. High Commissioner for Refugees and Unocal (which Corporate Watch refers to as 'a company with one of the worst human rights and environment records in the world.').

On the subject of partnerships between the U.N. and the private sector, Carol Bellamy, Executive Director of the U.N. Children's Fund (UNICEF, the U.N. agency with the most extensive corporate involvement), said recently that 'it is dangerous to assume that the goals of the private sector are somehow synonymous with those of the United Nations, because they most emphatically are not.' She said it is perfectly right and legitimate for business and the U.N. to be pursuing their different mandates, 'and when they can work as partners, so much the better.' She concluded: 'But in coming together with the private sector, the United Nations must carefully, and constantly, appraise this relationship.'[423]

Since June 1999 a number of corporations have sponsored food donations to the U.N.

World Food Program, the amount of each donation dependent on the number of people who each day 'hit' the 'Donate Free Food' button on the Food Program's online web page: http://www.thehungersite.com. The average corporate donation per day is around $400 (80,000 hits at $.005 each). The companies involved in this project receive publicity and advertising as a result of their participation; advertising boxes for the day's sponsoring companies (which if hit takes the computer user to the company's website) appear after the 'Donate Free Food' button is hit.[424]

The World Bank in 1997-98 helped to launch Business Partners for Development (BPD), 'an informal global network of business, government and civil society, with the World Bank Group as an equal partner, that aims to produce solid evidence of the positive impact of tri-sector partnerships – both the developmental impact and the business impact.'[425] The World Bank explained the thinking behind BPD:

Our starting point is the premise that there is growing pressure on companies to deliver, and demonstrate that they are delivering, value both to their shareholders and to the communities in which they operate. Corporate social responsibility is no longer an addition to the bottom line, but integral to it. New forms of partnerships are emerging that maximize the long term interest of the business sector along with the social and human development interests of the civil society and the state.[426]

Under the BPD program the World Bank and its more than 100 BPD partners are moving ahead with projects in four areas: youth development (coordinating partner: International Youth Foundation), water and sanitation (coordinating partner: WaterAid), natural resources (coordinating partner: CARE UK), and road safety (coordinating partner: International Federation of Red Cross and Red Crescent).[427] These projects 'aim to benchmark good practice and to develop impact evidence.'[428]

4. A slow response to the new realities

How should companies respond to allegations of human rights abuses? ■ How do corporations tend to respond in practice, and with what repercussions?

The trends discussed above in section 2 mean that companies will increasingly find human rights issues coming onto their agenda, whether they like it or not. Business is being warned about this; for example, in November 1998 Daniel Yergin, Chairman of Cambridge Energy Research Associates, told a meeting of the American Petroleum Institute that he considers one of the most important pressures on oil companies to be a long-term, growing emphasis on human rights and ethics.[429] Journalist Bennett Daviss noted in 1999: '[A] corporation will not be able to choose whether to have a social identity; the public will fashion one for it based on a company's social and environmental actions – or lack thereof.'[430]

But as the millennium approaches, most companies have still not come to terms with the new reality that they are to be held accountable for their human rights-related record. Most have not yet seriously addressed international human rights issues in their company policies and practices. As Sir Geoffrey Chandler notes:

Shell and BP have led the way in explicitly spelling out new human rights principles for their companies and a commitment to their implementation. Rio Tinto has followed these major players on the world scene. But the absentees – the American, German, French and Italian transnationals – remain in the majority, treating human rights violations as external to their responsibilities, regarding any adverse impact as a public relations problem rather than one that lies in the heart of the boardroom....[431] Concern for human rights appears to require corporate disaster or attritional external pressure to bring change, as did the slow corporate acceptance of protection of the environment.[432]

Looking back at the criticism Shell faced after the execution of Ken Saro-Wiwa and the Brent Spar incident, Shell's Senior Managing Director Cor Herkstroter acknowledged that Shell had 'become inward looking, isolated,'[433] and had been guilty of 'technological arrogance'[434] and insensitivity to the view of society.

In *When Good Companies Do Bad Things*, the authors identify why certain companies have failed 'to prevent bad things from happening' (including human rights crises):

■ *They fail to create a culture that tolerates dissent or one in which planning processes are encouraged to take nonfinancial risks seriously.*

■ *They focus exclusively on financial measures of performance.*

■ *They discourage employees from thinking about their work as whole people, from using their moral and social intelligence as well as their business intelligence.*

■ *They talk to the same circle of people and information sources all the time and avoid people or organizations who disagree with or criticize them.*

■ *They let their commitment to a particular project or product overwhelm all other considerations – financial, ethical, or social.*

■ *The senior managers consider ethical or social issues as matters for somebody else to resolve – a vice president for social responsibility, the United Nations, the host country government.*

In short, when companies have not examined their operations from a long-term perspective in a social context, they are much more vulnerable to the type of bad things we have described in this book (what author Ian Mitroff calls crisis-prone companies). We propose that once a company brings this perspective to its strategy development and operational planning, it will, of necessity, reperceive the issue of social responsibility and find many opportunities to turn that issue into a distinctive competency.[435]

Sir Geoffrey Chandler has noted that…

it is perhaps unsurprising that companies should fail so significantly in understanding the world in which they work. Technical and commercial success, the insulating carapace of high salaries, company transport, and corporate palaces shield senior executives from a world where non-governmental organisations (NGOs) and single-issue pressure groups, rather than politicians, now reflect the values of society and attract popular allegiance[436]*….From this viewpoint, the corporate instinct is to rebut, to look to public relations as a defence, not to change.*[437]

Peter Drucker also has recognised the fatal tendency of many companies to resist change:

Businesses that go unchallenged for long decades are rare exceptions. The great majority, no matter how successful, need to think through their basic assumptions much sooner. The great majority, moreover, then find it almost impossible to change.[438]

Drucker notes that over the past forty years only one-third of the 500 top manufacturing companies in the U.S. have managed to maintain their position, and those that did maintain their position 'had to change fundamentally.' He notes that one of the biggest threats to the survival of companies is 'complacency.'[439]

It is disappointing that so many companies that find themselves embroiled in a human rights controversy have repeated each other's mistakes. They do not seem to have learned from the experiences of other companies, and have paid for this failure with permanent damage to their reputation.

An intelligent company response to allegations of involvement in human rights abuses would be to:

i)   state that any involvement in abuses would be contrary to the company's policies (companies with explicit human rights policies can do this more persuasively);

ii) promise a prompt, thorough and impartial investigation;

iii) pledge that if any abuses are found, the company will take prompt action to remedy the situation and to prevent further abuses.

But most companies have started by denying the allegations and attacking the critics. Whether or not these companies believed the allegations to be true, were they so out of touch with societal attitudes towards human rights issues that they thought blanket denials and attacks on human rights advocates would stop the pressure? It tended to have the opposite effect. The company's next step often has been grudging recognition that something needs to be done, but too often it tries to get by with minimalist steps such as a half-hearted internal review that looks like a public relations exercise. This just prolongs the controversy and further damages the company's business and reputation. When the company finally (often years later) admits that mistakes had been made, agrees to take remedial action, and adopts human rights policies, shareholders should ask why the company had damaged itself by not taking these steps sooner, why the company's management allowed itself to be consumed for years by a human rights controversy that could have been avoided. If positive steps had been taken at the outset they would have been seen as acts of corporate leadership (and more importantly they could have stopped human rights abuses sooner); after so much delay they appear to be defensive moves, an exercise in damage control. Sir Geoffrey Chandler recently wrote:

Why [do] the boundaries of accepted responsibility have to be pushed forward by disaster and external pressure, rather than forethought and internal leadership? Is there an inherent incompatibility between corporate purpose and the valid expectations of society? …Why…do the transnational companies – some of the most sophisticated of organisations – require damage to reputation or a long attritional battle to force change?[440]

The Economist Intelligence Unit's *Business Asia* (a 'fortnightly report to managers of Asia operations') in 1997 issued a report entitled 'Just don't,' warning other companies to avoid the mistakes Nike had made:

Human and labour rights groups, along with the news media, bring images of underpaid, ill-treated workers – adults and children – into living rooms worldwide. In this instance, usually disinterested consumers might vilify a once loved brand name. It is this chain of events that makes company managers lose sleep at night: manufacturing decisions become subject to the force of public opinion.…

But the question remains, how can a company prevent, or at least detect and fix, a problem that might balloon into a PR nightmare?.…

Hindsight is of course 20:20 and Nike would doubtless prefer to have caught these problems before they became headline news.…In today's marketplace, consumers demand that brand leaders embody the virtues of social responsibility. Nike…would have done better to focus more resources and money on the early steps in the manufacturing of its products. Humanitarian issues aside, it is clear that one bout of bad publicity can undo hundreds of millions of dollars worth of marketing. Indeed a joyless marketing manager might point out it would have cost less to pay plant workers properly than to rebuild customers' good will.[441]

No doubt Shell has learned many lessons from its mistakes, and Nike has learned many lessons from its mistakes, and as the Economist Intelligence Unit says, 'they are better off for the lessons learned.'[442] But why had Shell not learned more from earlier mistakes by Freeport-McMoRan and Rio Tinto so that it could have avoided similar problems, and why had Nike not learned more from the experiences of The Gap and Shell? If the manage-

ment and directors of other companies are not now learning from what happened to Shell and Nike and acting on those lessons by proactively adopting and implementing human rights policies and reviewing their human rights practices, they are not doing their job on behalf of shareholders, and not fulfilling their responsibility to promote respect for human rights. They risk being added to the list of companies whose reputations have been damaged by a human rights controversy. As Sir Geoffrey Chandler notes, 'It was the absence of appropriate policies and practices which moved Shell and BP from the financial columns of the media to front page headlines for their actions in Nigeria and Colombia respectively.'[443]

Corporate public relations experts now are telling business that it is better to address human rights issues proactively and constructively rather than waiting to react when the company comes under attack. Hill & Knowlton, a U.S.-based public relations firm, advises companies to deal with labour issues constructively rather than defensively.[444] Referring favourably to Hill & Knowlton's advice to business, the Economist Intelligence Unit's *Business Asia* noted:

Many companies enter Asia without fully understanding the local business environment. Finding the cheapest contractor or partner may not be in the best interest of the firm. Hiring a local consultant to help a firm acclimatise is key. Advisors can help to proactively develop a strong relationship with unions, the local media and, most importantly, with workers.[445]

Sir Geoffrey Chandler urges companies to face up to human rights challenges with wisdom and leadership rather than defensively resisting the attention being focused on their social record:

For companies, scrutiny is here to stay as they acquire greater influence in a globalised world. They face two possible scenarios: they can resist the extension of the boundaries of their responsibilities, as they have in the past, so jeopardising their own reputations and – more dangerously – endangering the principle of the market system as a whole. Or they can demonstrate real corporate leadership which will underpin their economic contribution and raise their reputation. There are no other choices.[446]

5. A case in point: Nike

How did Nike respond to allegations of poor working conditions in its factories? ■ What has happened since Nike announced a new approach to human rights in May 1998?

During the past decade many companies facing human rights controversies have learned the hard lesson that human rights advocates, the media, and consumers will no longer be satisfied until they see real and verifiable change not only in company policy but also in company conduct. A case in point: Nike.

In 1996 accusations were made that Nike's Asian factories were sweatshops where workers were underpaid and mistreated. The allegations included:

i) salaries were less than required by local law and/or below subsistence level;

ii) working conditions were unsafe and protective clothing was lacking;

iii) forced overtime was used;

iv) workers were fired for becoming pregnant;

v) workers were prohibited from talking with co-workers;

vi) workers were fired for seeking to improve working conditions or for going on strike;

vii) a Taiwanese factory manager lined up 125 assembly-line workers and slapped them with the sole of an athletic shoe;

viii) a Korean factory manager made workers lick the factory floor as punishment; and

ix) workers at one factory were forced to run around three warehouses for punishment; a dozen fainted in the 100-degree heat.[447]

Nike's response over time was, like other companies that have faced human rights allegations, reactive and slow. Nike's response is summarised below as a four-stage process. Elaine Bernard, Executive Director of the Harvard Trade Union Program, has noted five common stages in a company's response to criticism of their social and labour record in developing countries:

i) **Denial:** The company denies any knowledge of human rights violations or denies that the violations are occurring. 'Most of their denials...include statements to the effect that 'we meet all the local standards, and are good employers.''

ii) **Blame others:** As the violations are corroborated, the company blames others for the shortcomings, perhaps their suppliers/ contractors, or the local government for its failures of enforcement, or the workers themselves for their failure to complain.

iii) **Damage control:** The company engages in damage control by taking the offensive and denouncing its critics who are labelled 'as 'zealots,' or 'troublemakers,' or 'publicity hounds.'...the claim is made that the critics have 'a political' or 'labor agenda.'' Sometimes the company threatens to bring a defamation lawsuit.

iv) **Reassert control over damaged corporate image:** The company attempts to recapture the high ground by establishing and publicising a code of conduct, often with assistance from a public relations firm.

v) **Give the appearance of compliance:** The company may seek to give the appearance of compliance and enforcement of the code of conduct by hiring auditing firms or high-profile monitors. Sometimes the company seeks to 'divide and conquer' its critics by splitting the human rights community between those who support this sort of monitoring and those who insist on more systematic, independent monitoring and enforcement.[448]

5.1 Stage 1: Deny allegations, attack critics

Nike started by strongly denying the allegations, saying it was a leader in improving working conditions in the developing world, offering 'highly-desirable jobs.'[449] The company said: 'Wherever Nike operates around the globe, it is guided by principles set forth in a Code of Conduct that binds its production subcontractors to a signed Memorandum of Understanding.'[450] Nike claimed that 'every Nike subcontractor is subject to systematic, unannounced evaluation carried out by Ernst & Young'[451] and that 'our own reviews, as well as Ernst & Young's, have shown that the Code [of Conduct] is complied with in all material terms....'[452] Nike also attacked its critics, saying:

i)   the allegations were organised by U.S. labour groups that didn't want to see jobs going overseas;

ii) its critics were citing outdated information; and

iii) organisations criticising Nike had suspect motives and were engaging in irresponsible criticism.[453]

5.2 Stage 2: Half-measures

As negative publicity continued, Nike joined Business for Social Responsibility, began a dialogue with the Robert F. Kennedy Center for Human Rights on how to ensure that the rights of workers are protected, and joined President Clinton's Apparel Industry Partnership (aimed at voluntarily working to assure consumers that goods are produced under acceptable labour conditions; see section 3.4).[454]

Then in 1997 Nike sent Andrew Young to investigate the alleged abuses. Young is a human rights leader, former U.S. ambassador to the U.N., and former mayor of Atlanta. He heads an Atlanta consulting firm, GoodWorks International. After Young's 15-day Asian tour of 12 Nike factories, he/GoodWorks International issued a report in June 1997 that

generally was favourable about Nike's record.[455] It did identify some problems and made some recommendations for improvement, e.g.:

i)   workers didn't know enough about their rights or about Nike's code of conduct;

ii) few factory managers spoke the local language, which inhibited workers from lodging complaints;

iii) Nike should promote the development of 'worker representatives';

iv) Nike should expand its dialogue with the human rights community and labour groups within the countries where they produce goods; and

v)   Nike should consider using independent monitors because factories are controlled by absentee owners and Nike had too few supervisors on site.

Young concluded that 'Nike is doing a good job in the application of its Code of Conduct, but Nike can and should do better.' He said he saw no evidence of 'systematic abuse or mistreatment' of workers and that Nike factories were 'clean, organized, adequately ventilated, and well-lit....I was expecting to see a far worse situation.' Young did not address the issue of wages, saying that he was not qualified to assess pay in a global economy, and that minimum wage standards need to be addressed by governments 'through national law or international standards.'[456]

Nike bought full-page ads in the *New York Times* and other major newspapers, drawing attention to the conclusions of the Young report.[457]

The Young report was strongly criticised by human rights groups and others for reasons including:

i)   it failed to address the issue of wages, not even making the point that Nike has a responsibility to pay a living wage;

ii) Young spent only 3 to 4 hours at each factory, the visits were pre-announced, and he did not re-visit any factories;

iii) Young's interviews with workers were conducted using Nike interpreters, and Young had no way of knowing whether the interpretation was accurate;

iv) The interviews with workers were conducted on the factory premises, leading two

Asian human rights organisations to comment:

Chinese workers do not know who Mr. Young is, and probably assumed he was part of the company. Workers naturally assume that a well-dressed foreign visitor who is introduced by management in the confines of the factory is connected to the company. In these circumstances, most workers would fear punishment if they shared their true feelings. Moreover, in our research, workers told us that management informs them beforehand when visitors are coming and asks them to behave well and clean up the work place. It would not be surprising if workers had been informed about Young's visit before his arrival. Under such circumstances, how can workers be expected to freely express their true concerns and feelings?;[458]

v)   Young and his consulting agency were paid by Nike for the report…both Young and Nike refused to disclose the amount paid; and

vi)   The report lists 34 NGOs that it says were consulted during the investigation, but in many cases there had been very little or no contact with those listed.[459]

The heavy criticism of Andrew Young's report confirmed that a company must do more than bring in a respected individual to examine its human rights record. The fact-finding process itself must be thorough and sound.

The pressure on Nike did not relent, indeed it accelerated in November 1997 when an internal report by Nike's auditing firm was leaked to the press by a disgruntled employee, resulting in front page coverage in the *New York Times*. The Ernst & Young report was based on a late 1996 audit of the Tae Kwang Vina factory in Vietnam; the report was delivered to Nike in January 1997 but kept secret until it was leaked to the media 10 months later. The report said that workers at a Nike factory in Vietnam were exposed to carcinogens that exceeded local legal standards by 177 times in parts of the plant, and that 77 percent of the employees suffered from respiratory problems. The report also stated that employees at the site had to work 65 hours a week, far more than Vietnamese law allows, for $10 a week.[460]

When the Ernst & Young report came to light, it led to further criticism of Andrew Young's report. Nike had received the Ernst & Young report in January 1997, but when Andrew Young went to Asia in March-April 1997 he did not even visit the Tae Kwang Vina factory in Vietnam, and did not address the serious health and safety issues in the Ernst & Young report. 'Either Nike withheld the Ernst & Young Tae Kwang Vina audit from Andrew Young, or Andrew Young and/or his staff negligently or recklessly ignored the Ernst & Young report.'[461]

In April 1998 a civil lawsuit was filed against Nike in the San Francisco, California, Superior Court, alleging that Nike had violated state law by misleading customers about the working conditions in its Asian factories. This was a 'private attorney general action' for 'unlawful and unfair business practices' that violate California's Business and Professions Code. Such cases can be brought in California state courts more easily than elsewhere in the U.S. because under California's broad consumer protection laws the plaintiff does not need to show that he or she personally suffered injury; it is enough to show that there was a likelihood of deception. The lead attorney said at the time of lodging the complaint, 'Nike has failed to tell Californians the truth about their business practices. They misrepresented the conditions in their factories and the wages they paid to protect their profits, and that's illegal.'[462] The press statement issued the day the complaint was filed said:

The most damning evidence against the company is contained in a 1997 Ernst & Young internal audit. Despite Nike's claims in a January 1996 letter that its Memorandum of Understanding certifies compliance with 'applicable government regulations regarding occupational health and safety [and] environmental regulations,' Ernst & Young's inspection of a Vietnamese Nike shoe plant found evidence of widespread health and safety violations.[463]

The purpose of the complaint was stated to be to get Nike 'to correct the discrepancy between its public rhetoric and its actual labor practices overseas….to force the company to bring its labor practices up to the level of its claims.'[464]

The complaint says that Nike misrepresented the truth when the company made claims including:

i) that Nike workers were not subjected to punishment or sexual abuse;

ii) that Nike products are made in accordance with laws governing wages and hours;

iii) that health and safety regulations are followed at Nike factories;

iv) that Nike pays average line-workers double the minimum wage in Southeast Asia;

v) that Nike workers receive free meals and health care;

vi) that the Andrew Young (GoodWorks International) report proves that Nike is doing a good job and 'operating morally';

vii) that Nike guarantees a 'living wage' for its workers.[465]

The complaint refers to extensive documentation that contradicts Nike's claims, including the above-mentioned Ernst & Young report. The complaint accuses Nike of violations of California law including negligent misrepresentation, fraud and deceit. It asks for Nike to turn over any profit made through unfair business practices and to undertake a corrective advertising campaign to explain how its products were produced.

The complaint was pending at the time Nike announced some changes to its policies in May 1998. The case was never argued on its facts; instead Nike moved for the complaint to be dismissed saying that even if the facts argued against it were true (which Nike did not accept) there would be no basis under law for finding Nike liable. Nike argued that its claims were made not in paid advertisements but in the context of statements to shareholders, over the internet, and to reporters, which Nike considered to be non-commercial speech protected by the First Amendment of the U.S. Constitution.[466] The Superior Court judge in February 1999 held in favour of Nike and dismissed the case, finding no legal basis for it to proceed.[467] The judge did not explain his precise reasons for dismissing the case; this is not required when a motion to dismiss is granted.[468] The case is being appealed by the plaintiffs, who argue in their appellate brief that Nike's statements about its labour practices were commercial speech intended to induce consumers to buy its products and that the lower court erred because the First Amendment does not protect commercial speech that is false, deceptive or misleading. The brief also argues that even if Nike's statements were noncommercial speech the action must be allowed to proceed because the First Amendment does not bar the action.[469]

5.3 Stage 3: Announcing change

In a May 1998 speech to the National Press Club, Philip Knight, Nike's Chairman and CEO, announced that Nike would tighten air quality standards at its overseas factories to meet the same standards as in the U.S., would raise the minimum age of its workers, and would allow independent local labour and human rights experts to participate in factory inspections (and publish summaries of their findings). When announcing these initiatives, he said:

It has been said that Nike has single-handedly lowered the human rights standards for the sole purpose of maximizing profits. The Nike product has become synonymous with slave wages, forced overtime and arbitrary abuse. I truly believe that the American consumer does not want to buy products made in abusive conditions.[470]

Human rights advocates welcomed this announcement, but expressed disappointment that there was no reference to the underlying issue of wages. They also cautioned that it would be important to wait to see how the independent inspections would be conducted and which organisations would be allowed to participate. Some advocates also noted that until there is more respect for freedom of association and freedom of expression in the countries where Nike locates its factories, workers will always risk reprisal if they speak up.[471]

5.4 Stage 4: Steps towards implementing change; more remains to be done

Nike reportedly has now introduced improvements in its Asian factories. Overtime has been reduced, new ventilation systems have been installed, lead-based paints and solvent-based adhesives have been eliminated. The number of workers at Tae Kwang Vina factory reporting nose and throat complaints reportedly fell to 18% of the labour force in 1998 from 86% in 1997.[472] There is a new system for workers to submit complaints and suggestions into a box for which only union representatives have a key.[473]

Human rights advocates recognise the progress that Nike has made in health and safety issues, but there is continuing concern about wage levels, and about how the factories will be monitored.

Nike has asked the International Youth Foundation (IYF), an NGO based in the U.S., to undertake work at Nike Asian factories to assess worker and community needs and devise projects for workers relating to education, health, nutrition, education, and vocational skills training.[474] The IYF is 'an independent, international, nongovernmental organization dedicated to the positive development of children and youth throughout the world.'[475] The IYF is to carry out this work through a new IYF division called The Global Alliance for Workers and Communities, a partnership of business, public and non-profit organizations founded by Nike, Mattel, the IYF, the World Bank, and the John D. and Catherine T. MacArthur Foundation. The primary goals of the Alliance are stated as follows:

■ *identify life aspirations and workplace issues based on research and worker feedback;*

■ *assess worker/community needs;*

■ *develop and implement programs to address these issues and worker aspirations and needs;*

■ *provide regular reports and updates to the public demonstrating results by company and country.*[476]

Phil Knight, Nike's CEO, made the following comment when The Global Alliance was launched:

We believe this initiative takes the right approach – it builds directly on input from workers themselves; it complements our existing independent monitoring

activities; and it creates an excellent platform through which Nike can make significant investments to improve the quality of life for its young adult workers throughout the world.[477]

Regarding factory monitoring, the IYF/Global Alliance is being asked to help 'build an improved ability to assess factory environments among local non-government organizations.'[478] The IYF/Global Alliance however emphasises that it is not a factory monitoring agency, that it will not be monitoring factory conditions, and that its focus will be on assessing the needs of workers.[479] Nike says the monitoring will involve international accounting company PriceWaterhouseCoopers:

Since 1994, Nike has required independent external third-party monitoring of our factories by international accounting organizations such as Ernst & Young (until 1998) and PriceWaterhouseCoopers. The Apparel industry Partnership and outside observers agree that this form of external monitoring, when coupled with NGOs, is an effective method to ensure compliance with Nike's code of conduct.[480]

Nike has signed on to the Apparel Industry Partnership's Fair Labor Association agreement (see section 3.4), so its factories will be subjected to an external monitoring process.

Human rights advocates will be closely scrutinising the various procedures for monitoring Nike's factories, to see how they work in practice. They are watching to see which local NGOs will be involved in the monitoring process, how they will be involved, and whether the fact-finding process is carried out with sufficient independence, expertise and thoroughness.

In early 1999 Nike became embroiled in controversy again. It was discovered that Joseph Ha, Nike Vice President and Special Assistant to Nike CEO Philip Knight, made the following remarkable statement in an 11 January letter to Cu Thi Hau, President of the state-run Vietnam General Confederation of Labour:

It was obvious that a few U.S. human rights groups, as well as a Vietnamese refugee who is engaged in human rights activities, are not friends of Vietnam. Their ultimate goal is political rather than economic. They target Nike because Nike is a high profile com-

pany and a major creator of jobs in Vietnam. Nevertheless, this is the first step for their political goal which is to create a so-called 'democratic' society, modeled after the U.S. No nation needs to copy any other nation. Each nation has its own internal political system. Nike firmly believes in this.[481]

A senior executive at Nike was denouncing human rights groups just after the international community had called for an end to attacks on human rights defenders. In December 1998 Amnesty International joined other human rights organisations and human rights defenders from over 100 countries (including Wei Jingsheng and Nobel laureates José Ramos Horta and the Dalai Lama) in Paris for the first-ever world summit of human rights defenders. Amnesty International's Secretary General Pierre Sané said: 'I think all those who contributed to the conception of the UDHR [Universal Declaration of Human Rights] in 1948 would be horrified to listen to the personal testimonies from these brave individuals gathered here who have been persecuted by their governments merely for peacefully trying to defend the rights set out in that historic document.' He said that human rights defenders were 'ordinary people around the world who have shown extraordinary courage by taking it upon themselves to defend the rights of others.'[482]

Also in December 1998 the U.N. General Assembly adopted an historic declaration recognising the important role played by human rights defenders. That declaration states that everyone has the right, individually and in association with others, to gather information on human rights and to disseminate that information.[483]

The letter from Nike's Joseph Ha apparently was intended to be kept private, but became public when the Vietnam General Confederation of Labour published it in its official newsletter. Following its publication (and subsequent reporting about the letter in the news media including via BBC radio to Vietnam), Thuyen Nguyen, the Vietnamese-American who heads Vietnam Labor Watch, found that his sources about labour conditions inside Vietnam dried up. Thuyen Nguyen explains:

With this accusation, Nike has taken the protest into the political arena. And politics is not something most Vietnamese want to get involved [in] because politics is too hard to predict and sometimes can be detrimental to one's life and livelihood. As long as we can keep this on the labor issue, we can find people who are willing to help us monitor these factories. People who have been helping us have been doing it out of their desire to improve the factories. But by equating monitoring Nike factories with being political extremists, Nike has made [it] dangerous for these people.[484]

Human rights organisations that sit with Nike on the White House Apparel Industry Partnership (the Lawyers Committee for Human Rights, the National Consumers League, the Robert F. Kennedy Memorial Center for Human Rights, and the International Labor Rights Fund) expressed serious concern about the 'anti-democratic and authoritarian values' reflected in Joseph Ha's letter. These organisations called on Nike to take the following corrective steps:

The only way that Nike can recover its integrity in this matter is to reverse publicly, in Vietnam, its position and make clear to the Vietnamese government and the Vietnam General Confederation of Labor that Nike values the work of human rights monitors in general and that, in particular, it recognizes and respects the positive work of the Vietnam Labor Watch organization headed by Mr. Thuyen Nguyen. For this step to carry sufficient weight, it is necessary for Nike to encourage Mr. Thuyen Nguyen publicly to continue his important advocacy work in Vietnam, and to accompany him in meetings with Vietnamese officials to correct the wrong done to him by the letter from Joseph Ha. It is also important that Dr. Ha be sanctioned sufficiently by Nike, by demotion, dismissal or transfer, to convey convincingly to a skeptical public that he did not, in fact, speak for Nike, only for himself.[485]

Nike responded by sending a letter to these organisations that said:

Nike's position on this letter is perfectly clear – the views expressed in the letter were Dr. Ha's and Dr. Ha's alone; they do not represent the position of Nike and are inconsistent with what we have been saying and doing as a company. This position has been articulated in news media interviews, and in a pub-lished letter to the Financial Times which ran the first account of this matter.

We do not believe that one remark by one executive in a private exchange should be the basis on which our key relationships with the NGO community are pred-icated.[486]

On 24 February 1999 Nike Vice President of Law & Corporate Affairs Lindsay Stewart sent a letter to Cu Thi Hau (President of the Vietnam Confederation of Labour, recipient of the 11 January letter from Nike's Joseph Ha). Her let-ter included the following comments:

We would like to make it clear that the views expressed in that letter [from Joseph Ha] were Dr. Ha's and Dr. Ha's alone; they do not represent the position of Nike and are inconsistent with what we have been saying and doing as a company. Because his job responsibil-ities do not and will not include working with NGOs, we would like to clarify Nike's position....Over the years, Nike has learned a great deal from a variety of NGOs in many different countries. We value our rela-tionships with all of the organizations [with] which we have had dialogue and developed partner-ships....We believe NGOs play an important role in the promotion of human and labor rights around the world. While we do not always see eye-to-eye with some of these groups, we have learned from them, respect their views, and recognize their right to exist and to express their views freely. This is the case with Vietnam Labor Watch – a U.S. based organization which we believe, like others, is dedicated to improving working conditions for workers within Vietnam. We will continue to seek dialogue and build relationships with NGOs as we develop our labor and community programs in Vietnam. We have found these partner-ships extremely valuable, [they] bring greater efficien-cy to our work, and positive impact to people in the factories and their communities....A copy of this letter is being sent to the Lao Dong newspaper.[487]

Joseph Ha reportedly remains in his position at Nike.[488] Joseph Ha's letter – a formal business letter apparently on Nike letterhead from a Nike Vice President (reportedly one of only two Special Advisors to Nike CEO Phil Knight) to an official in another country – must surely have been perceived by the Vietnamese recipi-ent as representing the views of Nike.

If as Nike says Joseph Ha's letter did not reflect the company's thinking, it is difficult to understand how a man so senior in the compa-ny could have been so out of touch with the company's high profile, highly publicised new approach to human rights. Whether or not Joseph Ha's letter reflected Nike's thinking, the incident is a reminder that when a company commits itself to a human rights policy, that commitment needs to be internalised into its corporate culture. Announcing a new policy is not enough. The practical implications of the new policy must be explained to all manage-ment and staff at headquarters and overseas. This requires training of company employees to raise their level of awareness about human rights and to give them guidance on how the principles should be applied in their day-to-day work. The company's human rights policies need to be backed up with a system of reporting and accountability that ensures adherence is strictly enforced.

Whether or not Joseph Ha's letter in fact reflected Nike's thinking, the strong public reaction to its disclosure reflects a long-stand-ing concern that while companies tend to endorse social responsibility in their public statements, sometimes company officials may be sending a very different message in their day-to-day work and private exchanges. This concern is reflected in the public's scepticism when business people say they prefer 'quiet diploma-cy' as a method for raising human rights issues with governments. Human rights advocates recognise that sometimes it is important for companies and governments to discuss such issues out of the public spotlight. But in the past 'quiet diplomacy' has too often been used by companies as an excuse to do nothing at all about human rights and to avoid accountability. An intelligent company, if it wants to, can find ways to make its support for human rights and the rule of law known through both public and private means, without jeopardising its ability to continue operating in a country. Particularly sensitive issues of course may need to be raised with tact and subtlety, or by a group of compa-nies rather than a single one. While fundamen-tal internationally-recognised human rights are universally applicable across all cultures, multinational companies should be culturally sensitive in the time, place and manner of raising human rights issues, and should acknowledge that human rights violations occur in their home country as well. But cultural sensitivity should never be an excuse for inaction, and private discussions should never be a company's only means of addressing human rights concerns. When 'quiet diplomacy' is used, the burden is on business people to convince doubters that such private discussions are in fact taking place and that the right issues are being raised.

In October 1999, Nike became the first large apparel company to disclose the names and locations of overseas factories which make athletic gear carrying the names of U.S. universities (see section 3.4 of this report for details).

Business Week magazine reported in November 1999 that Press for Change, the New Jersey-based labour rights advocacy group, had just completed a survey of 2300 workers at five Nike factories in Indonesia employing 45,000 people. In the survey's interviews (conducted by an Indonesian human rights NGO), more than half of the workers said they had seen colleagues yelled at or mistreated, and a third said they had been compelled to work overtime. *Business Week* reported that Nike spokesman Vada Manager said the company had not yet seen the survey but would look into the matter.[489]

6. A dialogue with business

What are the main issues arising in discussion with business people about human rights?
■ Does the Universal Declaration of Human Rights reflect Western values or global values?
■ Why do business managers prefer human rights recommendations to be country-specific?

During the past several years I have had the opportunity to discuss business and human rights issues with managers from a number of multinational corporations. Following are my impressions and some of the subjects that arose in these discussions:

6.1 Universality of human rights versus cultural relativism

When it came to a discussion of international human rights standards, the threshold questions posed by business people were important ones that required considerable discussion: Does the Universal Declaration of Human Rights reflect Western values that they should not impose on countries with other cultural traditions? Have non-Western countries accepted the Universal Declaration? Has China accepted the Universal Declaration?

In response to these questions it was important first to stress the need for cultural sensitivity in deciding the time, place and manner of raising human rights issues, as well as the need to recognise that one's home country also has human rights shortcomings. But it was also important to emphasise that human rights by their very definition are universal and internationally-recognised. Business people were genuinely surprised to hear that virtually every country in the world is on record expressing support for the Universal Declaration of Human Rights, and to hear that China had not only endorsed the Universal Declaration but also had ratified the U.N. Convention against

Torture. They were impressed by statements of Asians and Africans about being offended by the suggestion that the right to life, freedom from torture, the prohibition of arbitrary detention, and the right to a fair trial are just Western values. Principles of the sacredness of life, of human dignity, and of the importance of justice and fair treatment are reflected in the teaching of all religions and all cultures. The full text of my explanation to business people of the universality of human rights will be available online in late 1999 or early 2000.[490]

6.2 Business' responsibility to promote human rights

Business people were interested to hear that corporations have a responsibility under international standards to promote respect for human rights. I drew their attention to the passage in the Universal Declaration of Human Rights stating that 'every individual and every organ of society' has the responsibility to strive 'to promote respect for these rights and freedoms' and 'by progressive measures, national and international, to secure their universal and effective recognition and observance.'[491] As important institutions of society, companies have a responsibility to promote worldwide respect for international human rights. As Sir Geoffrey Chandler has observed, the Universal Declaration 'not only legitimizes a company's right to speak out on such matters: it imposes an obligation to do so.'[492]

It was also important to draw attention to the fact that international business leaders have recognised the private sector's responsibility to respect and promote human rights, for example in 'The Caux Round Table Principles for Business.'[493]

6.3 Economic, social and cultural rights

I found it important on many occasions, especially when there was some hesitation by a business person to see any connection between the private sector and human rights, to point out that their company had probably been engaged with some human rights issues for many years. I explained that economic, social and cultural rights were part of the Universal Declaration of Human Rights, and therefore any effective community programmes their company had supported in fields such as sustainable development, education, or health were promoting human rights. That would lead to a discussion about the need for the company to address the full range of human rights, including civil and political rights, since human rights are interdependent.

6.4 Lawsuits

Business people were interested to learn about human rights-related lawsuits that had been brought against corporations, and the damage those lawsuits had caused to the reputation of companies.

6.5 Diverse levels of human rights awareness and attitudes

Some of the managers were very attuned to human rights issues, while to others the subject was something very foreign to their experience. Those who worked in a country with a high level of human rights concerns were not necessarily more knowledgeable about human rights issues than their colleagues working in Western Europe or North America.

I found most discussions among company managers about human rights to be lively affairs reflecting a diversity of views: these were issues they knew could affect them and their company. Some of the managers spoke passionately about their own commitment to human rights and their anxiety about specific abuses taking place in countries where they operated, while other managers (particularly those who were citizens of the country where the alleged human rights violations were taking place) tended to defend the government's point of view (without defending the government's alleged abuses).

6.6 Business managers working overseas want human rights guidelines

No matter what a manager's level of awareness or attitude about human rights, all managers working in countries with a high level of human rights concerns wanted from company headquarters clearer, practical guidelines on what they should be doing to ensure the company's overseas operations respect human rights, and on how they should handle human rights issues arising either within the company or externally. They did not want their company headquarters to think that by adopting a broad set of human rights principles they had washed their hands of the matter; they wanted to know exactly how the company wanted them to behave on the ground in relation to real human rights issues. They had seen what had happened to Shell in Nigeria, to BP in Colombia and to Nike in Asia, and they did not want to find themselves held responsible for getting their company into a similar situation.

6.7 Country-specific human rights recommendations

Managers working in a particular country or region were not fully satisfied with the generic recommendations on business and human rights produced by Amnesty International and other NGOs. While they found many of the general principles articulated in those guidelines to be useful, they considered some of the recommendations to be too broad or not fully relevant or realistic in relation to the particular part of the world where they worked. I tried to assist by producing two country-specific sets of guidelines, one for China and one for Colombia.[494] These country-specific recommendations were drawn in part from recommendations put forward by Amnesty

International and other international human rights organisations, with the addition of recommendations tailored to the particular country.

6.8 Difficult issues for business

The discussions kept coming back to several dilemmas: How can we do business in a country where human rights violations are widespread without being perceived as being too close to the government or profiting from the repression? If we must work in a joint venture with the government, and rely on the government's security forces to protect our staff and operations, and if those security forces allegedly have committed human rights violations, what can we do? Human rights organisations want us to use our influence to promote human rights and the rule of law...how can that be done without jeopardising our ability to continue doing business in the country? At what point would (or should) a high level of human rights abuses by the government cause us to withdraw from the country?

7. Companies in the developing world: Projects promoting human rights

What are the shortcomings in many company-supported social programmes? ■ What standards of good practice have been developed to assist companies? ■ How are some companies promoting civil and political rights? ■ Are NGOs interested in working with business?

In 1996 and 1997 I travelled to South Africa, India, Thailand and the Philippines to look at what business is doing to promote development and human rights in the wider society. In each country I met with companies, development organisations and human rights organisations, and saw a number of the initiatives that were underway. My findings:

7.1 Varying track records

In each country I visited I found some very impressive business-supported projects promoting sustainable development, education, health, poverty alleviation, environmental protection, child welfare, women's issues, and civil/political rights. The best programmes I saw were aimed at helping people and communities become economically self-sufficient, rather than providing charity and creating dependency. Many of the best programmes were partnerships between companies and development organisations, human rights organisations, and/or local communities. Some of the better projects I saw, and others I did not see, are described in case examples presented in two books:

i)   *Business as Partners in Development: Creating wealth for countries, companies and communities*, by Jane Nelson/The Prince of Wales Business Leaders Forum, in collaboration with The World Bank and The U.N. Development Programme;[495] and

ii) *Foundations for a New Democracy: Corporate Social Investment in South Africa*, by Myra Alperson.[496]

However, I also found that many companies are doing very little. One reason for the shortcomings is that corporate community programmes promoting development and human rights receive relatively little external scrutiny and therefore are given relatively low priority within many companies.

In some cases company community programmes have been criticised as misguided and ineffective. In South Africa the *Mail and Guardian* newspaper publishes once or twice a year a supplement entitled 'Investing in the Future: Special Focus on Corporate Responsibility.' Its October 1997 supplement highlighted some of the better community projects supported by South African companies, but also contained an article entitled 'Corporate do-gooding 'suspect'', [497] written by Horst Kleinschmidt, Executive Director of the Kagiso Trust[498] (a large South African NGO which promotes grassroots development programmes). He wrote that he considers corporate social investment programmes in South Africa to be, in terms of their output and relevance to development, 'in the main, inappropriate, inadequate and often thoroughly misguided':

First, it is my impression that South African corporates who have a CSI [corporate social investment] programme play their cards extremely close to their chests. Very often it is the chairman's (and I empha-

sise man in this connection, because he is a man and invariably a white man) domain to decide who will get what kind of support. The knowledge or understanding of the development needs of the recipients eludes him in general. Far too often this type of chairman is far more motivated by the publicity his company may attract, or the photo opportunity it may give him, than the real developmental need....

My greatest concern is that most corporates cannot distinguish between publicity for themselves, charity handouts and developmental objectives. The upshot is a mélange of confused thoughts, mixed with the desire to impress the government that they are doing something and hoping thus to stave off government's inclination to legislate what companies might do with their CSI contribution....

[W]hat eludes most corporates is any sense of commitment in their CSI. Most of it is cheque-book project support. The notion of involvement with a beneficiary community eludes most corporates. Where it exists it is mostly of a patronising kind. I have come across few companies that see their CSI as an encounter through which they learn about the environment in which they live and understand better the appalling gap between rich and poor in this country.

[A]ll CSI programmes that engage management and staff in a debate on the purpose and meaning of CSI and then proceed to outline what the company may be doing in relation to potential beneficiaries, begin to tackle the CSI debate seriously.[499]

Horst Kleinschmidt concluded that in South Africa the corporate sector, NGOs and the government need to engage with one another more closely 'for the better exchange of ideas and experiences in the CSI and development field.' In particular, he urged companies and NGOs to work as partners, rather than behaving 'as though they are ships passing in the night, the one not aware of or caring about the other.' He noted that this increased co-operation should not aim to 'cajole anyone into one development straightjacket,' but rather the 'starting point should be: development is difficult and we all make mistakes. What are we learning in the process and what can we do to ensure that our collective effort, diverse as it is

and will remain, contributes to real development and real reconstruction?'[500]

A 1999 book edited by the Federation of Indian Chambers of Commerce and Industry includes a chapter that recognises the achievements of company-supported social programmes in India, but also acknowledges shortcomings:

Though there is undoubtedly greater interest in becoming better corporate citizens, few companies take their commitment seriously enough to make an annual allocation, earmarking a defined percentage of their profits. Very few have a proper strategy and plan of work, and community betterment is yet to be integrated into mainstream operations. Companies have yet to professionalize their community betterment work, much of which suffers from ad hocism. And forming partnerships [with NGOs] is still an exception rather than a norm.[501]

There is a pressing need for sustained independent monitoring of this area of corporate performance, in order to give more public recognition to those companies that are making a meaningful contribution, and to provide an incentive for other companies to do likewise. Such monitoring should assess corporate programmes both quantitatively and qualitatively.

7.2 Organisations promoting business partnerships for development

Some of the best company-supported social projects are being facilitated by organisations that assist member companies to form partnerships with NGOs and communities, and that promote 'best practice' aimed at ensuring projects are implemented effectively. These organisations include:

i)   India: Partners in Change/ActionAid[502]

ii) India: Business Community Foundation (formerly India Business and Community Partnership)/The Prince of Wales Business Leaders Forum[503]

iii) Philippines: Philippine Business for Social Progress (PBSP)[504]

iv) South Africa: National Business Initiative (NBI)[505]

v)   Thailand: Thai Business Initiative in Rural Development (TBIRD)[506]

7.3 Standards of good practice

The aforementioned publication *Business as Partners in Development* (see section 7.1), in a chapter entitled 'Learning from 'good practice,'' sets forth and explains the following factors that have been crucial to the success of multi-stakeholder partnerships involving companies:

i)   Clear and common goals based on mutual benefit;
ii) Role of intermediary leadership;
iii) Understanding and consulting beneficiaries and stakeholders;
iv) Clarity of roles and responsibilities;
v)   Understanding resource needs and capacities;
vi) Communication;
vii) Evaluating and celebrating progress; and
viii) Continuous learning and adaptation.[507]

The Center for Corporate Community Relations at Boston College has published 'The Standards of Excellence in Community Relations: Guiding Principles for Community Relations Practice' a set of benchmarks for corporations to use in developing their community programmes.[508]

As discussed in section 2.6, Oxfam has set forth six principles for accountable development derived from internationally-recognised human rights standards.[509]

In a 1999 issue of *Harvard Business Review*, Harvard Business School Professor Rosabeth Moss Kanter discusses six characteristics of successful business-government and business-NGO partnerships aimed at addressing social issues: 'a clear business agenda, strong partners committed to change, investment by both parties, rootedness in the user community, links to other community organizations, and a long-term commitment to sustain and replicate the results.'[510]

7.4 Indigenous companies leading the way

I found that corporations with the most extensive and innovative programmes tended to be indigenous companies rather than multinationals from Western Europe or North America, though some of the multinational companies also have excellent projects underway.

7.5 Varying support for projects promoting civil and political rights

In South Africa and the Philippines a number of companies are willing to sponsor programmes aimed at promoting civil and political rights as well as economic, social and cultural rights. For example, in the Philippines the Ayala Foundation (the foundation of the Ayala Corporation) has backed an important initiative, the Barangay Human Rights Action Program.[511] Under this programme, the Ateneo Human Rights Center organises human rights experts to train local 'human rights officers' who then help people at the grassroots level learn about and protect their civil, political, economic, social and cultural rights. The human rights officers also help resolve conflicts by mediation and conciliation. One component of the initiative is human rights training of the police. The programme is also supported by the national Commission on Human Rights and the Philippines Government. A joint statement by the President of Ayala Corporation and the Executive Director of the Ayala Foundation explained that Ayala considered this human rights project to be important because it is 'a step in giving the poor better access to better justice.'[512]

In India and Thailand many companies support ambitious development projects, but for various reasons they are somewhat reluctant to support programmes promoting civil and political rights. There are signs that this may be slowly changing, for example in Thailand several corporations are now sponsoring Pollwatch, the respected independent organisation working to ensure fair elections and to stop vote-buying by politicians.

7.6 Non-governmental organisations' attitudes towards working with business

The vast majority of the development and human rights organisations I met in the four countries were either already working in partnership with companies in some of their projects, or were eager to do so. Partly this is a matter of economic survival, because in a country like South Africa aid to NGOs from Europe and

North America has been drying up since the end of apartheid, and many of the most respected NGOs are struggling financially while they try to address overwhelming needs. Of course NGOs do insist on certain preconditions for working in partnership with a company on a project, to ensure that the project is not commercialised, and to ensure the company is committed to carrying out the project in a way that addresses the real needs of the beneficiaries. They also want to avoid working with a company that may be supporting a project with the aim of covering up its poor record of exploiting workers or damaging the environment. Several NGOs told me that under no circumstances would they work with the private sector, but these represented a relatively small proportion of a broad spectrum of NGOs I encountered.

7.7 Companies and the social agenda

Another issue of concern is whether companies involved in social programmes may try to take over the agenda or dilute the message. Companies do not have a democratic mandate to direct the social agenda, and are not subject to democratic accountability. While this risk needs to be borne in mind and guarded against, in the countries I visited the problem had not tended to arise much in practice, partly because NGOs and governments were aware of the risk, and partly because most companies recognised their limitations in the social arena and showed little eagerness to take control.

7.8 Globalisation: A threat to company-supported social development programmes?

An important question arose during my trip to India: How will globalisation impact the ambitious rural development projects sponsored by some Indian corporations? A case in point: Tata, India's largest industrial conglomerate, comprising about 85 companies.[513] Since its founding in the 1800s Tata has had a reputation for social responsibility, and its rural development projects reach thousands of villages throughout India, including isolated tribal communities. Some Tata companies have hired leading NGO experts in rural development to run their community programmes.

But Tata increasingly has to compete with multinationals coming into India, and many of those multinationals will not have the same commitment as Tata to social programmes aimed at the development of India. Drucker notes that 'every knowledge organisation is of necessity non-national, non-community.'[514] Lester Thurow agrees:

For the first time in human history, anything can be made anywhere and sold everywhere. In capitalistic economies that means making each component and performing each activity at the place on the globe where it can be most cheaply done–and selling the resulting products or services wherever prices and profits are highest....Sentimental attachment to some geographic part of the world is not part of the system.[515]

Social critic Charles Derber noted recently: 'The multinational corporation has become less geographically anchored than ever before, prospering with diminishing loyalty to individual workers, communities, and the nation-state itself.'[516] Multinationals can move anywhere and won't necessarily feel any deep ties to the places where they locate their operations.

Will Tata be forced to cut back its rural development programmes because of increasing competition with multinationals? Will globalisation mean companies have to reduce their development and human rights programmes to the lowest common denominator? Or can a way be found to encourage multinationals coming into the Indian market to learn lessons from Tata in terms of their social contribution?

8. Conclusion

Does globalisation impose greater demands on companies with regard to human rights? ■ Why is there a backlash against globalisation, and what steps can business take to limit this?

As globalisation accelerates, the human rights performance of companies will be more closely scrutinised, evaluated and compared. Each company must now decide whether it will face up to human rights challenges with wisdom and leadership, or will defensively resist the attention being focused on its social record. Companies can no longer sit on the sidelines of the debate; inertia and inaction will be deemed irresponsibility. Superficial public relations gestures and codes of conduct that are not implemented or independently monitored will be seen for what they are. Companies will be expected to treat human rights issues with the same seriousness they give to traditional business issues, not as an afterthought or a damage-control exercise. A human rights component must be integrated into the company's decision-making at all levels — it must be on the agenda, for example, when deciding: whether to invest or locate in a country, where to locate in a country and the impact that may have on existing communities, issues to raise with a host government, how to approach environmental/health/safety measures, how to deal with workers' organisations and to ensure they are allowed to operate in full freedom, recruitment/training/compensation/promotion/working hours of managers and staff, how to deal with allegations of discrimination or sexual harassment, how to deal with strikes or demonstrations against the company, security arrangements, what community projects should be supported by charitable giving. Companies that pay serious attention to respecting and promoting human rights will see their reputations enhanced. Those that do not will see their reputations suffer.

It is not just the reputations of individual companies that are at stake for the private sector. A backlash against globalisation and the market system is growing, largely because of dislocations and inequities caused by the new world economy, but also due to irresponsible behaviour by some multinational corporations, and a perception that too many multinational corporations address social, human rights and environmental concerns only if forced to do so and then only minimally. In December 1997 the Workplace Editor of *Business Week* magazine referred to 'a growing backlash against globalisation around the world.'[517]

In June 1999 U.N. Secretary-General Kofi Annan, speaking to the Chamber of Commerce of the U.S., said: 'As you know, globalization is under intense pressure. And business is in the line of fire, seen by many as not doing enough in the areas of environment, labour standards and human rights.'[518] The fact sheet on the Secretary-General's proposed 'Global Compact' notes that the 'backlash against liberalization' could lead to a 'return to market protectionism and unnecessary barriers against technical and commercial innovation.' The document concludes: 'To be sustainable, globalization must be accompanied by the effective promotion and protection of human rights, labour standards and the environment.' [519]

The Director-General of the International Labour Office, Juan Somavia, said in an address to business leaders in November 1999: 'Globalization has brought both prosperity and inequalities, which are testing the limits of collective social responsibility. If we are to avoid a serious backlash against the process of globalization, concerted action is needed.' He urged business to be 'part of the solution by addressing issues of equity, human dignity and labour rights, and by lifting those who are in danger of being left behind.'[520]

Lester Thurow concludes in *The Future of Capitalism* that the private sector and the capitalist system must find a way to address social needs in a meaningful way if they are to survive and succeed:

If capitalism is to work in the long run, it must make investments that are not in any particular individual's immediate self-interest but are in the human community's long-run self-interest. How does a doctrine of radical short-run individualism emphasize long-run communal interests? How can capitalism promote the values that it needs to sustain itself when it denies that it needs to promote any particular set of values at all? Put simply, who represents the interests of the future to the present?[521]

Endnotes

1 P. Drucker, *Post-Capitalist Society* (New York: HarperBusiness, 1993).

2 Ibid., p. 8.

3 L. Thurow, *The Future of Capitalism* (New York: Penguin Books, 1996), p. 8.

4 Ibid., pp. 66-67.

5 Recent books/articles raising questions or concerns about the effects of globalisation include: W. Allmand/International Centre for Human Rights and Democratic Development, 'Trading in Human Rights: The Need for Human Rights Sensitivity at the World Trade Organization' (Mar. 1999); S. Anderson, et al., *Field Guide to the Global Economy* (New York: New Press, forthcoming Feb. 2000); S. Beder, *Global Spin: The Corporate Assault on Environmentalism* (White River Junction, Vermont: Chelsea Green Publishing Co., 1998); C. Caufield, *Masters of Illusion: The World Bank and the Poverty of Nations* (New York: Henry Holt & Company, Inc., 1997); M. Chossudovsky, *The Globalisation of Poverty: Impacts of IMF and World Bank Reforms* (London: Zed Books Ltd., 1997); Christian Aid/M. Lockwood and P. Madden, 'Closer Together, Further Apart: A discussion paper on globalisation' (Sept. 1997), <http://www.christian-aid.org.uk/f_reports.htm>, accessed on 28 July 1999; Christian Aid/A. Wood and M. Lockwood, 'The Perestroika of Aid? New Perspectives on Conditionality' (Mar. 1999), <http://www.christian-aid.org.uk/f_reports.htm>, accessed on 28 July 1999; J. Fox and L. Brown, eds., *The Struggle for Accountability: The World Bank, NGOs and Grassroots Movements* (Cambridge, Massachusetts: The MIT Press, 1998); T. Friedman, *The Lexus and the Olive Tree: Understanding Globalization* (New York: Farrar, Straus and Giroux, 1999); J. Gray, *False Dawn: The Delusions of Global Capitalism* (New York: The New Press, 1998); W. Greider, *One World, Ready or Not* (New York: Touchstone/Simon & Schuster, 1997); Harvard Law School Human Rights Program, *Business and Human Rights: An Interdisciplinary Discussion Held at Harvard Law School in December 1997* (Cambridge, Massachusetts: Harvard Law School Human Rights Program, 1999); International Centre for Human Rights and Democratic Development/D. Bronson and S. Rousseau, 'Working Paper on Globalization and Workers' Human Rights' (26 Oct. 1995), <http://www.ichrdd.ca/PublicationsE/apecen.html>, accessed on 11 Aug. 1999; C. Jochnick, 'The Human Rights Challenge to Global Poverty' (Feb. 1999), Center for Economic and Social Rights website ('publications'), <http://www.cesr.org/>, accessed on 11 Aug. 1999; J. Karliner, *The Corporate Planet: Ecology and Politics in the Age of Globalization* (San Francisco: Sierra Club Books, 1997); D. Korten, *When Corporations Rule the World* (West Hartford, Connecticut: Kumarian Press, 1995; San Francisco: Berrett-Koehler Publishers, 1995); E. Lee, *The Asian Financial Crisis: The challenge for social policy* (Geneva: International Labour Office, 1998); C. LeQuesne, *Reforming World Trade: The Social and Environmental Priorities* (Oxford: Oxfam Publications, 1996); J. Madeley, *Big Business, Poor Peoples: The Impact of Transnational Corporations on the World's Poor* (London: Zed Books, 1999); J. Mander and E. Goldsmith, eds., *The Case against the Global Economy* (San Francisco: Sierra Club Books, 1996); Oxfam Policy Department, *A Case for Reform: Fifty Years of the IMF and World Bank* (Oxford: Oxfam Publications, 1995); R. Papini, et al., eds., *Living in the Global Society* (Aldershot, England: Ashgate Publishing, 1997); D. Rodrik, *Has Globalization Gone Too Far?* (Washington, D.C.: Institute for International Economics, 1997); D. Rodrik, *The New Global Economy and Developing Countries: Making Openness Work* (Washington, D.C.: Overseas Development Council, 1999); S. Sassen and K. Appiah, *Globalization and Its Discontents: Essays on the New Mobility of People and Money* (New York: New Press, 1999); G. Soros, 'The Capitalist Threat,' *Atlantic Monthly* (Feb. 1997), <http://www.theatlantic.com/issues/97feb/contents.htm>, accessed on 28 May 1999; G. Soros, 'Toward a Global Open Society,' *Atlantic Monthly* (Jan. 1998), pp. 20-32; G. Soros, and G. Shandler, ed., *The Crisis of Global Capitalism: Open Society Endangered* (New York: PublicAffairs, 1998); A. Taylor and C. Thomas, eds., *Global Trade and Global Social Issues* (London: Routledge, 1999); K. Thanawala, 'Promoting Justice in the International Economy: Role of the Church,

Governments and Business' (undated, Villanova University), <http://www.stthomas.edu/cath-studies/cstm/antwerp/p24.htm>, accessed on 11 Aug. 1999; K. Thanawala, 'Toward a Just World Economy,' *Review of Social Economy* XLIX (1991), pp. 628-37; L. Thurow, *The Future of Capitalism, supra* n. 3; K. Watkins, *Economic Growth with Equity: Lessons from East Asia* (Oxford: Oxfam Publications, 1998); J. Wiseman, ed., *Alternatives to Globalisation: An Asia-Pacific Perspective* (Fitzroy, Victoria, Australia: Community Aid Abroad, 1997).

6   J. Garten, 'Globalism Doesn't Have to be Cruel,' *Business Week* (9 Feb. 1998).

7   Drucker, *Post-Capitalist Society, supra* n. 1, p. 57.

8   Ibid., pp. 80, 97, 101.

9   U.N., Universal Declaration of Human Rights, <http://www.unhchr.ch/udhr/index.htm>, accessed on 23 May 1999.

10   U.N. World Conference on Human Rights, The Vienna Declaration and Programme of Action, adopted 25 June 1993, Art. 5, <http://www.unhchr.ch/html/menu5/d/vienna.htm>, accessed on 23 May 1999.

11   World Commission on Environment and Development, *Our Common Future* (Oxford: Oxford University Press, 1987).

12   M. Friedman, 'The Social Responsibility of Business Is to Increase Its Profits,' *New York Times Magazine* (13 Sep. 1970).

13   J. Welch, Jr., 'A CEO Forum: What Corporate Social Responsibility Means to Me; Wanted: Teachers and Leaders,' *Business and Society Review*, No. 81 (spring 1992), p. 88.

14   Tata Council for Community Initiatives, Statement by Ratan Tata at meeting of Tata Council for Community Initiatives, 8 May 1996.

15   JRD Tata letter inviting Justice Mr S P Kotwal to head the Social Audit Committee of Tata Steel, 1979, quoted in Tata Community Initiatives, 'Social accounting and auditing: Why social accounting?' (undated).

16   J. Makower, *Beyond the BottomLine* (New York: Simon & Schuster, 1994), p. 13.

17   Ibid., pp. 31-32.

18   Ibid., p. 23.

19   'Green light for partnership,' *The Shield Magazine: The international magazine of the BP Group*, Issue One (1998), pp. 34-35.

20   G. Soros, 'The Capitalist Threat,' *The Atlantic Monthly*, Vol. 279, No. 2 (Feb. 1997), <http://www.theatlantic.com/issues/97feb/capital/capital.htm>, accessed on 1 Nov. 1998.

21   Royal Society for the encouragement of Arts, Manufactures and Commerce, *Tomorrow's Company: The role of business in a changing world* (Aldershot, Hampshire, England: Gower, 1995), p. 1, *see also* the 'Tomorrow's Company' website: <http://www.tomorrowscompany.com/>, accessed on 8 June 1999; M. McIntosh, et al., *Corporate Citizenship: Successful Strategies for Responsible Companies* (London: Financial Times/Pitman Publishing, 1998), p.47.

22   Royal Society for the encouragement of Arts, Manufactures and Commerce, *Tomorrow's Company, supra* n. 21, p. iii.

23   Ibid., p. ii.

24   Ibid., p. 10.

25   Ibid.

26   L. Wah, 'Treading the Sacred Ground,' *Management Review* (July/Aug. 1998), p. 21.

27   Ibid.

28   P. Schwartz and B. Gibb, *When Good Companies Do Bad Things: Responsibility and Risk in an Age of Globalization* (New York: John Wiley & Sons, 1999), p. xi; Telephone interview with staff at Columbia University Graduate School of Business, 13 Aug. 1999.

29   C. Marsden, Warwick Business School Corporate Citizenship Unit, 'Human rights teaching in Business schools,' *Human rights & Business matters* (Amnesty International UK Business Group Newsletter) (spring 1999), p. 4.

30   Asian Institute of Management, *Center for Development Management* (undated).

31   Ibid.

32   Royal Dutch/Shell, 'Statement of General Business Principles' (1997), <http://www.shell.com/principles/general_a.html>, accessed on 24 May 1999.

33   Royal Dutch/Shell, *The Shell Report 1999: People, planet & profits: An act of commitment* (1999), <http://www.shellreport.com>, accessed on 28 Apr. 1999.

34   Ibid., p. 2.

35   'Announcing The Next Bottom Line: Agenda for the 21st Century,' *Business Week* (1 Mar. 1999), p. 17.

36   C. M. Armstrong, 'A Global Alliance for the 21st Century,' in special advertising section ('The Next Bottom Line'), *Business Week* (3 May 1999).

37   J. Lash, 'The New Millenium and the Next Bottom Line,' introduction to special advertising section ('The Next Bottom Line'), *Business Week* (3 May 1999).

38   'The Dayton Hudson Foundation' and '50+ Years of Giving,' <http://www.dhc.com/dhf/index.htm>, accessed on 31 May 1999.

39 Human Resources Network, *An Evaluation of the Dayton Hudson Giving Program* (21 Mar. 1983).

40 J. Elkington, *Cannibals with forks:The triple bottom line of 21st century business* (Oxford: Capstone Publishing, 1997), p. 125.

41 Drucker, *Post-Capitalist Society, supra* n. 1, p. 80.

42 Ibid., p. 101.

43 Ibid., p. 97.

44 U.N. General Assembly, United Nations Declaration on the Right to Development, adopted 4 Dec. 1986, Art. 6(2), <http://www.unhchr.ch/html/menu3/b/74.htm>, accessed on 22 May 1999.

45 The Vienna Declaration and Programme of Action, *supra* n. 10, Art. 10.

46 'A Government by the People: Kim Dae Jung on what he wants for his country,' *Time (Asia Edition)*, Vol. 151, No. 8 (2 Mar. 1998), <http://cgi.pathfinder.com/time/asia/magazine/1998/980302/qa.html>, accessed on 10 Apr. 1998.

47 A. Sen, 'Economics and the value of freedom,' *Civilization: The Magazine of the Library of Congess* (June/July 1999), p. 84, <http://www.civmag.com/>, accessed on 12 Aug. 1999.

48 C. Forcese, *Profiting From Misfortune? The Role of Business Corporations in Promoting and Protecting International Human Rights*, MA Thesis, Norman Paterson School of International Affairs, Carleton University, Ottawa (1997), referred to in C. Forcese, *Putting Conscience into Commerce: Strategies for making human rights business as usual* (Montréal: International Centre for Human Rights and Democratic Development, 1997), p. 18.

49 OECD, *Trade, Employment and Labour Standards*, COM/DEELSA/TD(96)8/FINAL (1996), p. 42; referred to in Forcese, *Putting Conscience into Commerce, supra* n. 48, p. 18. The OECD study examined 38 emerging markets and found that 15 countries made improvements in free association after making trade reforms; 9 countries made such improvements before making trade reforms; 8 countries made such improvements at the same time as making trade reforms; 6 countries made no such improvements before, during or after trade reforms.

50 OECD, *Trade, Employment and Labour Standards, supra* n. 49, p. 47, referred to in Forcese, *Putting Conscience into Commerce, supra* n. 48, p. 18.

51 Forcese, *Putting Conscience into Commerce, supra* n. 48, p. 19.

52 D. Orentlicher and T. Gelatt, 'Public Law, Private Actors: The Impact of Human Rights on Business Investors in China,' 14 *Northwestern Journal of International Law & Business* (1993), pp. 100-101, referred to in Forcese, *Putting Conscience into Commerce, supra* n. 48, pp. 19-20.

53 Amnesty International, *China: No one is safe – An Amnesty International Briefing*, AI Index ASA 17/02/96 (Mar. 1996).

54 J. Allen, *The Essential Desmond Tutu* (Cape Town: David Philip Publishers/Mayibuye Books, 1997), pp. 39-40.

55 Aung San Suu Kyi, 'Empowerment for a Culture of Peace and Development' (address delivered on her behalf at a Nov. 1994 meeting of UNESCO's World Commission on Culture and Development and at a Dec. 1994 forum for Democratic Leaders in the Asia-Pacific), in Aung San Suu Kyi, *Freedom from Fear and other writings* (London: Penguin Books, 1995), p. 267.

56 'Burma's Suu Kyi: Take your investments elsewhere, please,' *Business Week* (30 Mar. 1998).

57 Canadian Friends of Burma (CFOB), *Dirty Clothes-Dirty System* (Ottawa, CFOB, 1996), p. 51, referred to in Forcese, *Putting Conscience into Commerce*, p. 18.

58 Forcese, *Putting Conscience into Commerce, supra* n. 48, pp. 22-24.

59 *New York Times* (6 Dec. 1998).

60 C. Fombrun, *Reputation: Realizing Value from the Corporate Image* (Boston: Harvard Business School Press, 1996), pp. 10, 32.

61 Ibid., pp. 5-6, 8-9.

62 J. Nelson/The Prince of Wales Business Leaders Forum, *Business as Partners in Development: Creating wealth for countries, companies and communities* (London: The Prince of Wales Business Leaders Forum, 1996), pp. 47, 52.

63 G. Chandler, 'Human rights have everything to do with business,' *The Observer* (U.K.) (19 May 1996).

64 G. Chandler, 'People and profits,' *The Guardian* (14 Nov. 1996).

65 BP, *BP Social Report 1997* (1998), p. 1.

66 Elkington, *Cannibals with forks, supra* n. 40, p. 110.

67 Forcese, *Putting Conscience into Commerce, supra* n. 48, p. 12.

68 International Centre for Human Rights and Democratic Development (ICHRDD), 'Globalisation, Trade and Human Rights: The Canadian Business Perspective,' Summary report, Conference held on 22 Feb. 1996, in Toronto, Canada,

<http://www.ichrdd.ca/PublicationsE/repo-sum.html>, accessed on 18 Mar. 1999.

69 Reebok, *Reebok Human Rights Production Standards*, <http://www.reebok.com/human_rights.html>, accessed on 23 May 1999.

70 J. Ayala II, 'Philanthropy Makes Business Sense,' *Business Day* (Bangkok) (25 Sep. 1995); J. Ayala II, 'Philanthropy Makes Business Sense,' *Ayala Foundation Inc. Quarterly* Vol. 4, No. 2 (July-Sep,Oct-Nov 1995), p. 3.

71 David Lewin is the Neil Jacoby Professor of Management, Organizational Behavior and Human Resources at the Anderson Graduate School of Management at UCLA (University of California – Los Angeles).

72 D. Lewin and J. M. Sabater, 'Corporate Philanthropy and Business Performance,' *Philanthropy at the Crossroads* (Bloomington, Indiana: University of Indiana Press, 1996), pp. 105-126.

73 Ibid, p. 124.

74 Ibid, pp. 118-125.

75 C. Verschoor, 'A Study of The Link Between a Corporation's Financial Performance and Its Commitmnt to Ethics,' *Journal of Business Ethics* (Oct. 1998), p. 1515.

76 R. Kanter, 'From Spare Change to Real Change: The Social Sector as Beta Site for Business Innovation,' *Harvard Business Review* (May-June 1999), p. 124.

77 'From austerity to prosperity: Profile, Bangchak Petroleum managing director Sophon Suphaphong,' *Bangkok Post* (11 Dec. 1996), 'Outlook' section, p. 1.

78 A. Panyarachun, 'Human Rights and Business Ethics,' International Symposium on Human Rights and Business Ethics (24 Oct. 1998), Bangkok, <http://www.thaiembdc.org/pressc-tr/statemnt/others/hr_102498.htm>, accessed 18 Mar. 1999.

79 B. Daviss, 'Profits from Principle: Five Forces Redefining Business,' *The Futurist* (Mar. 1999), p. 30.

80 Centre for Tomorrow's Company, 'What is Tomorrow's Company?' <http://www.tomor-rowscompany.com/whatis_intro.html>, accessed on 20 Sep. 1999.

81 Wah, 'Treading the Sacred Ground,' *Management Review*, supra n. 26, p. 19.

82 Elkington, *Cannibals with forks*, supra n. 40, pp. 151-52.

83 J. Kennedy, 'API: Petroleum execs face non-market hurdles,' *Oil & Gas Journal* (16 Nov. 1998), pp. 36-37.

84 P. Sutherland, address to Amnesty International event, Dublin (26 Sep. 1997),

pp. 2-3, <http://www.bpamoco.com/speech-es/sp_9709.htm>, accessed on 27 May 1999.

85 Ibid., pp. 6-7.

86 J. Browne, 'Corporate Responsibility in an International Context,' address to Council on Foreign Relations, New York, 17 Nov. 1997, p. 6, <http://www.bpamoco.com/_nav/pressof-fice/speech.htm?>, accessed on 18 Apr. 1999.

87 BP Amoco, 'On the side of Human Rights,' <http://www.bpamoco.com/human rights/article.htm>, accessed on 23 May 1999.

88 Business for Social Responsibility, 'Human Rights: Business Importance,' <http://www.bsr.org/resourcecenter/>, accessed on 5 June 1999.

89 Amnesty International, 'ASEM: A human rights agenda for ASEM II (Asia-Europe Meeting), 3-4 April 1998, London' (AI Index 01/03/98, Feb. 1998), p. 4.

90 Schwartz and Gibb, *When Good Companies Do Bad Things*, supra n. 28, pp. 78-79.

91 Thurow, *The Future of Capitalism*, supra n. 3, p. 281.

92 Ibid., p. 280.

93 Drucker, *Post-Capitalist Society*, supra n. 1, p. 80.

94 P. Drucker, *Drucker on Asia: A dialogue between Peter Drucker and Isao Nakauchi* (Oxford: Butterworth-Heinemann, 1997), p. 128.

95 Drucker, *Post-Capitalist Society*, supra n. 1, pp. 66.

96 'Center Study Shows Good Image Boosts Employee Loyalty,' *Corporate Community Relations Letter*, Vol. 10, No. 2 (Oct. 1995), pp. 1,3.

97 'The Importance of Good Corporate Citizenship,' *The Wirthlin Report*, Vol. 5, No. 9 (Oct. 1995), p. 1.

98 Schwartz and Gibb, *When Good Companies Do Bad Things*, supra n. 28, p. 64.

99 See, for example, Human Rights Watch, *The Price of Oil: Corporate Responsibility and Human Rights Violations in Nigeria's Oil Producing Communities* (Jan. 1999), <http://www.hrw.org/hrw/reports/1999/nige-ria/index.htm>, accessed on 27 May 1999.

100 Information about the arrest, detention, trial and execution from Amnesty International, *Amnesty International Report 1996* (London: Amnesty International Publications, 1996), pp. 237-38.

101 Royal Dutch/Shell, *Profits and Principles – does there have to be a choice?* (1998), p. 16.

102 E. Imomoh, General Manager: Eastern Division, Shell Petroleum, on *Africa Express*, Channel 4 TV, UK (18 Apr. 1996), quoted in McIntosh, et al., *Corporate Citizenship*, supra n. 21, p. 123.

103 G. Chandler, 'Exploitation is our responsibility,' *Sunday Business* (U.K.) (16 Aug. 1998); G. Chandler, 'Oil Companies and Human Rights,' *Oxford Energy Forum* (Nov. 1997), p. 3.

104 Elkington, *Cannibals with forks, supra* n. 40, p. 8.

105 Wah, 'Treading the Sacred Ground,' *supra* n. 26, p. 18.

106 'Survey: Human-Rights Law; The power of publicity,' *The Economist* (5 Dec. 1998), p. 13.

107 R. Reich, 'The New Meaning of Corporate Social Responsibility,' *California Management Review* (Winter 1998), p. 10.

108 E&P Forum (The Oil Industry International Exploration & Production Forum, London), MORI-conducted opinion poll (1995).

109 Royal Dutch/Shell, *Profits and Principles, supra* n. 101, p. 2.

110 Sutherland, address to Amnesty International, *supra* n. 84, p. 9.

111 The Center for Corporate Community Relations at Boston College, 'Consumers Reward Social Responsibility, Finds Center Study,' *Corporate Community Relations Letter* (Dec. 1994), pp. 1-2.

112 S. McFadden, *Garment Workers Study* (Arlington, Virginia: Marymount University Center for Ethical Concerns, ICR Survey Research Group, 1995), cited in D. Spar, 'Foreign Investment and Human Rights,' *Challenge* (Jan.-Feb. 1999), p. 72, fn. 43.

113 D. Birnbaum, 'Forget MFN, the Consumers Are Coming!' *Wall Street Journal* (9 Apr. 1996).

114 S. Wollenberg/Associated Press, 'PepsiCo Pulls Out of Burma' (27 Jan. 1997); J. Mathews (*Washington Post* staff writer), 'Pepsi to sell Burma Plant, Citing Protests' (24 Apr. 1996), <http:www.soros.org/textfiles/burma/pepsi_wash.txt>, accessed on 27 May 1999.

115 The Center for Corporate Community Relations at Boston College, 'Surveys Say…Consumers more aware of social performance,' *Corporate Community Relations Letter* (July/Aug. 1995), p. 5.

116 Ibid.

117 Fruitman Consulting Group, *An Exploration of the Feasibility of a 'Clean Clothers' Programme in Canada* (Study conducted for the Ontario District of UNITE, 1995). Available from the Union of Needle Trades, Industrial and Textile Employees (UNITE), Toronto; referred to in Forcese, *Putting Conscience into Commerce, supra* n. 48, p. 36.

118 Universal Declaration of Human Rights, *supra* n. 9, preamble.

119 U.N., International Covenant on Civil and Political Rights, preamble, <http://www1.umn.edu/humanrts/instree/b3ccpr.htm>, accessed on 6 June 1999; U.N., International Covenant on Economic, Social and Cultural Rights, preamble, <http://www1.umn.edu/humanrts/instree/b2esc.htm>, accessed on 6 June 1999.

120 International Labour Office, Governing Body, Working Party on the Social Dimensions of the Liberalization of International Trade, 'Further examination of questions concerning private initiatives, including codes of conduct,' Doc. GB.274/WP/SDL/1 (Mar. 1999), para. 8, <http://www.ilo.org/public/english/20gb/docs/gb274/sdl-1.htm>, accessed on 19 May 1999.

121 U.N., 'The Global Compact,' <http://www.un.org/partners/business/fs1.htm>, accessed on 30 July 1999; see also U.N., 'The Global Compact,' <http://www.un.org/partners/business/globcomp.htm>, accessed on 15 Nov. 1999.

122 Ibid.

123 Ibid.

124 U.N., 'Business leaders advocate a stronger United Nations and take up challenge of Secretary-General's Global Compact' (5 July 1999), <http://www.un.org/partners/business/iccun1.htm>, accessed on 30 July 1999.

125 U.N., 'Statement by Mary Robinson, United Nations High Commissioner for Human Rights: Giving a Human Face to the Global Market – The Business Case for Human Rights' (WinConference '99, Interlaken, 10 June 1999), <http://www.un.org/partners/business/hchr-stat.htm>, accessed on 30 July 1999.

126 United Nations Declaration on the Right to Development, *supra* n. 44, Art. 2(2).

127 Ibid., Art. 3(3).

128 U.N. Commission on Human Rights, 'Globalization and its impact on the full enjoyment of all human rights,' resolution 1999/59, <http://www.unhchr.ch/Huridocda/Huridoca.nsf/TestFrame/b9f7cf403384cb27802567660047d603?Opendocument>, accessed on 27 Oct. 1999.

129 U.N. Sub-Commission on Prevention of Discrimination and Protection of Minorities, 'Globalization and its impact on the full enjoyment of all human rights,' resolution 1999/29, <http://www.unhchr.ch/Huridocda/Huridoca.nsf/TestFrame/c8ccf8b4eeac6226802567ed0054ec5c?Opendocument>, accessed on 27 Oct. 1999.

130 U.N. Sub-Commission on Prevention of Discrimination and Protection of Minorities, 'The relationship between the enjoyment of economic, social and cultural rights and the right to development, and the working meth-

ods and activities of transnational corporations,' resolution 1998/8, U.N. Doc.
E/CN.4/1999/4, E/CN.4/Sub.2/1998/45
(1998), p. 30, <http://www.unhchr.ch/huri-
docda/huridoca.nsf/0811fcbd0b9f6bd5802566
7300306dea/02f03447db7e5f5a8025667200577
8e8?OpenDocument>, accessed on 27 Oct.
1999.

131 U.N. Sub-Commission on Prevention of
Discrimination and Protection of Minorities,
'Report of the sessional working group on the
working methods and activities of transnational corporations on its first session,' U.N. Doc.
E/CN.4/Sub.2/1999/9 (12 Aug. 1999), paras.
32-34,
<http://www.unhchr.ch/Huridocda/Huridoca.
nsf/TestFrame/8fd5a0232e3c2a68802567d600
3b1143?Opendocument>, accessed on 21 Oct.
1999.

132 U.N. Sub-Commission on Prevention of
Discrimination and Protection of Minorities,
'Human rights and income distribution,' resolution 1998/14, U.N. Doc. E/CN.4/1999/4,
E/CN.4/Sub.2/1998/45 (1998), p. 42,
<http://www.unhchr.ch/huridocda/hurido-
ca.nsf/0811fcbd0b9f6bd58025667300306dea/8
48c2659041ed9b28025667200598987?OpenDo
cument>, accessed on 27 Oct. 1999; U.N. Sub-
Commission on Prevention of Discrimination
and Protection of Minorities, 'The Social
Forum,' resolution 1999/10,
<http://www.unhchr.ch/Huridocda/Huridoca.
nsf/TestFrame/2738057e702de311802567e000
319473?Opendocument>, accessed on 27 Oct.
1999>.

133 U.N. Sub-Commission on Prevention of
Discrimination and Protection of Minorities,
'Trade liberalization and its impact on human
rights,' resolution 1999/30, para. 1,
<http://www.unhchr.ch/Huridocda/Huridoca.
nsf/TestFrame/fd0ad067cc91f1a1802567ed005
51e7e?Opendocument>, accessed on 27 Oct.
1999.

134 U.N., *Report of the World Summit for Social
Development*, U.N. Doc. A/CONF.166/9 (1995),
Annex I (Copenhagen Declaration on Social
Development).

135 Ibid., Annex II (Programme of Action of the
World Summit for Social Development), para.
83(d).

136 Ibid., para. 12(e).

137 ILO, 'Tripartite Declaration of Principles concerning Multinational Enterprises and Social
Policy,' adopted Nov. 1977, para. 1,
<http://www.ilo.org/public/english/85multi/t
ridecl/index.htm>, accessed on 23 May 1999.

138 Ibid.

139 Ibid., para. 2.

140 Ibid., para. 8.

141 International Labour Conference, 'ILO
Declaration on fundamental principles and
rights at work' (June 1998),
<http://www.ilo.org/public/english/10ilc/ilc8
6/com-dtxt.htm>, accessed on 23 May 1999.

142 OECD, 'OECD Guidelines for Multinational
Enterprises,'
<http://www.oecd.org/daf/cmis/cime/mne-
text.htm>, accessed on 11 May 1999.

143 Ibid.

144 OECD, 'Development Partnerships in the New
Global Context,'
<http://www.oecd.org/dac/htm/dpngc.htm>,
accessed on 20 May 1999.

145 Ibid.

146 OECD, 'Shaping the 21st Century: The
Contribution of Development Co-operation,'
<http://www.oecd.org/dac/pdf/stc.pdf>,
accessed on 22 May 1999.

147 Ibid.

148 European Parliament resolution A4-0508/98,
'Code of conduct for European enterprises
operating in developing countries,' adopted
Jan. 1999, full text at <http://www.multination-
als.law.eur.nl/documents/cmp/coc99.html>,
accessed on 27 May 1999; see also Department
of Public Law, Erasmus University Rotterdam,
'European Parliament's Decision on MNCs,'
<http://www.multinationals.law.eur.nl>,
accessed on 27 May 1999.

149 'Peter Frankental, project manager of the
Business Group of Amnesty International UK,
asks Richard Howitt MEP about the significance of the European Parliament's resolution,' *Human rights & Business matters* (Amnesty
International UK Business Group Newsletter)
(spring 1999), p. 2.

150 'Government action on responsible business,'
Human rights & Business matters (Amnesty
International UK Business Group Newsletter)
(spring 1999), p. 3.

151 Ibid.

152 Department for International Development
(DFID), *Partnerships with Business*, p. 1.

153 The Netherlands Ministry of Foreign Affairs,
Explanatory Statement on the 1998 Budget,
Second Chamber of the States General, 1997-
1998, no. 25600, Chapter V, no. 2, referred to
in The Dutch Sections of Amnesty
International and Pax Christi International,
Multinational Enterprises and Human Rights
(1998), pp. 19-20.

154 U.S. Government, 'Model Business Principles'
(May 1995).

155 C. Chandler, 'Code of Conduct: Draft Assailed: Rights Groups Criticize Administration's Rules for US Firms Abroad,' *New York Times* (28 Mar. 1995), p. D4; C. Forcese, *Commerce with conscience? Human Rights and Corporate Codes of Conduct* (Montréal: International Centre for Human Rights and Democratic Development, 1997), p. 60, endnote 1.

156 Forcese, *Commerce with conscience? Human Rights and Corporate Codes of Conduct, supra* n. 155, p. 60, endnote 1.

157 'Government responds to call for federal task force on sweatshops,' Press release issued by NGOs following 11 May 1999 meeting to discuss sweatshop issues (11 May 1999).

158 Excerpt from remarks by President Nelson Mandela at launch of National Business Initiative (Mar. 1995), in National Business Initiative, 'Enhancing the Business Contribution to Make our Society Work for All' (undated).

159 Excerpt from remarks by President Nelson Mandela to the World Economic Forum Southern Africa Economic Summit, referred to in World Economic Forum, 'Presidents Mugabe and Mandela appeal for efforts to globalize sub-saharan Africa at the World Economic Forum's international business summit in Harare, Zimbabwe' (21 May 1997), <http://www.weforum.org/publications/press _releases/zaes97_globalize210597.asp>, accessed on 1 June 1999; e-mail from L. Stott, Prince of Wales Business Leaders Forum, 31 Mar. 1998.

160 Amnesty International, 'Human Rights Principles for Companies' (AI Index ACT 70/01/98, Jan. 1998).

161 Amnesty International, 'Nigeria: Time to end contempt for human rights' (AI Index AFR 44/14/96, 6 Nov. 1996), p. 25.

162 Amnesty International, 'Human rights are everybody's business' (AI Index ASA 17/18/96), Jan. 1996.

163 Chandler, 'Oil Companies and Human Rights,' *supra* n. 103, p. 4.

164 G. Chandler, 'The New Corporate Challenge: Globalization requires companies to do more than seek higher profits,' *Time* (1 Feb. 1999), p. 68, <http://cgi.pathfinder.com/time/reports/dav os/corp_challenge.html>, accessed on 3 Apr. 1999.

165 Human Rights Watch, 'Working Guidelines on Business and Human Rights' (June 1997).

166 Human Rights Watch, *Mexico – No Guarantees: Sex Discrimination in Mexico's Maquiladora Sector* (Aug. 1996), <http://www.hrw.org/hrw/sum-maries/s.mexico968.html>, accessed on 27 May 1999.

167 Human Rights Watch, *Mexico – A Job or Your Rights: Continued Sex Discrimination in Mexico's Maquiladora Sector* (Dec. 1998), <http://www.hrw.org/hrw/reports98/women2 />, accessed on 27 May 1999.

168 Human Rights Watch, *Colombia: Human rights concerns raised by the security arrangements of transnational oil companies* (Apr. 1998), <http://www.hrw.org/hrw/advocacy/corpora-tions/colombia/index.htm>, accessed on 27 May 1999.

169 Human Rights Watch, *The Enron Corporation: Corporate Complicity in Human Rights Violations* (1999), <http://www.hrw.org/hrw/reports/1999/enro n/>, accessed on 26 May 1999.

170 Ibid., p. 4.

171 Human Rights Watch, *The Price of Oil, supra* n. 99.

172 Global Exchange, 'Global Economy: China: What It's All About,' <http://www.globalex-change.org/economy/corporations/china/ove rview.html>, accessed on 4 Nov. 1999; Global Exchange, 'US Business Principles for Human Rights of Workers in China,' <http://www.globalexchange.org/economy/co rporations/china/principles.html>, accessed on 4 Nov. 1999; S. Billenness/Trillium Asset Management, 'New Initiatives on China and Tibet,' *Investing for a Better World* (Oct. 1999), p. 7.

173 U.N. World Conference on Human Rights, NGO Forum Final Report (June 1993), Working Group D, recommendation 30 and Working Group 5, recommendation 3, in R. Reoch (ed.), *Human Rights: The new consensus* (London: Regency Press, 1994), pp. 230-51.

174 The Interfaith Center on Corporate Responsibility, The Ecumenical Council for Corporate Responsibility, and The Taskforce on the Churches and Corporate Responsibility, *Principles for Global Corporate Responsibility: Bench Marks for Measuring Business Performance* (29 May 1998).

175 Ibid.

176 Council on Economic Priorities, 'CEPAA – A General Introduction,' <http://www.cepaa.org/intro.htm>, accessed on 18 Aug. 1999; McIntosh, et al., *Corporate Citizenship, supra* n. 21, pp. 246-49.

177 Council on Economic Priorities, *Shopping for a Better World* (San Francisco: Sierra Club Books, 1994); Council on Economic Priorities, 'Screen: Corporate Social Responsibility Research Service For Investors' ; Council on Economic Priorities,

'Global Screen'; The Council on Economic Priorities, *The Corporate Report Card: Rating 250 of America's Corporations for the Socially Responsible Investor* (New York: Dutton/Penguin, 1998).

[178] Council on Economic Priorities, *Tenth Annual Corporate Conscience Awards* (1996).

[179] World Monitors, <http://www.worldmonitors.com>, accessed on 22 Sep. 1999.

[180] Xi Mi, 'Business code helps to raise ethics,' *China Daily* (Beijing) (24 Oct. 1995).

[181] 'California Global Corporate Accountability Project,' <http://www.nautilus.org/cap/index.html>, accessed on 6 June 1999.

[182] Ibid., 'Bay Area Groups to Examine Human Rights and Environmental Claims of California High Tech and Oil Companies,' <http://www.nautilus.org/cap/news/pr011499.html>, accessed on 6 June 1999.

[183] ICHRDD, 'Globalisation, Trade and Human Rights,' *supra* n. 68.

[184] Forcese, *Putting Conscience into Commerce, supra* n. 48, pp. 8-9.

[185] 'Ethical Trading Initiative,' <http://www.ethicaltrade.org>, accessed on 25 May 1999.

[186] P. Feeney, 'New development agenda,' in Reoch (ed.), *Human Rights: The new consensus, supra* n. 173, p. 35.

[187] 'Quito Declaration…On the enforcement and realization of economic, social, and cultural rights in Latin America and the Caribbean' (24 July 1998), para. 17, Center for Economic and Social Rights website ('publications'), <http://www.cesr.org/>, accessed on 11 Aug. 1999.

[188] Ibid., paras 87-90.

[189] Center for Economic and Social Rights, 'About CESR,' <http://www.cesr.org/about.htm>, accessed on 12 Aug. 1999.

[190] C. Jochnick, 'The Human Rights Challenge to Global Poverty' (Feb. 1999), sec. IV-A, Center for Economic and Social Rights website ('publications'), <http://www.cesr.org/>, accessed on 11 Aug. 1999.

[191] Partners in Change/ActionAid, 'Corporate Partnership: Making Social Responsibility Work' (brochure describing the work of Partners in Change).

[192] Ibid.

[193] P. Feeney, *Accountable Aid: Local Participation in Major Projects* (Oxford: Oxfam Publications, 1998).

[194] Ibid., pp. 146-49.

[195] G. Chandler, 'Do the Right Thing,' *Green Futures* (Mar./Apr. 1999), p. 23.

[196] Ibid.

[197] The Fund for Peace, 'The Fund for Peace Foreign Policy Roundtable' (undated one-page description); 'The Fund for Peace Foreign Policy Roundtable: Report on a Dialogue Between Representatives of the Human Rights and Corporate Communities' (Jan. 1999).

[198] Amnesty International, 'Business and human rights: Mutual responsibilities, converging agendas,' speech given to the Keidanren by Rory Mungoven, Asia-Pacific Program Director of Amnesty International, Tokyo (27 Feb. 1998).

[199] Remarks by Pierre Sané, Secretary General of Amnesty International, Offshore Northern Seas 13th International Conference and Exhibition, Stavenger, Norway (25-28 Aug. 1998).

[200] Telephone interview with G. Crijns, Business Coordinator, Amnesty International Dutch Section, 14 Apr. 1999.

[201] BP, *BP Social Report 1997* (1998).

[202] Royal Dutch/Shell, *The Shell Report 1999: People, planet & profits, supra* n. 33, p. 28.

[203] 'Localities with Burma Selective Purchasing Laws,' <http://www.soros.org/burma/citylist.html>, accessed on 2 Apr. 1999.

[204] Ibid.

[205] Ibid.

[206] S. Billenness, 'Companies Take to the Courts: Case Against Burma Law Now Likely' (15 Apr. 1998), <http://soros.org/burma/le41598.html>, accessed on 2 Apr. 1999.

[207] Ibid.

[208] USA*Engage, <http://www.usaengage.org>, accessed on 2 Apr. 1999.

[209] M. Kelly, 'U.S. companies doing business in Myanmar are protest targets,' *Star Tribune* (Minneapolis) (27 May 1996), <http://danenet.wicip.org/fbc/files/article20.html>, accessed on 6 June 1999; Free Burma Coalition, 'PepsiCo and Burma,' <http://danenet.wicip.org/fbc/pepsi.html>, accessed on 6 June 1999.

[210] R. Mokhiber and R. Weissman, 'Sanctioning Burma, Sanctioning the United States,' *Focus on the Corporation* (23 Dec. 1997), <http://www.essential.org/monitor/focus/focus.9707.html>, accessed on 2 Apr. 1999; 'Advocates vow boycott of companies in Myanmar', *Journal of Commerce*, <http://www.joc.com/>, accessed on 2 Apr. 1999.

[211] S. Billenness, 'Burma Law on Trial: Case Threatens Anti-Apartheid Legacy,' *Investing for a Better World* (Apr. 1999), p. 1.

212 'Advocates vow boycott of companies in Myanmar', *supra* n. 210.

213 Telephone interview with S. Billenness, Trillium Asset Management, 20 Apr. 1999; 'Burma government follows ruling on Massachusetts boycott law,' *Boston Globe* (6 Nov. 1998), <http://shweinc.com/news/19981106-3.shtml>, accessed on 2 Apr. 1999.

214 Billenness, 'Burma Law on Trial,' *supra* n. 211, p. 1.

215 'EU files brief with US District Court in Massachusetts,' The European Union Press Releases, No. 65/98 (8 July 1998), <http://www.eurunion.org/news/press/1998-3/pr65-98.htm>, accessed on 2 Apr. 1999.

216 Mokhiber and Weissman, 'Sanctioning Burma, Sanctioning the United States', *supra* n. 210.

217 USA*Engage, 'Amicus Briefs Filed in Support of the National Foreign Trade Council,' <http://www.usaengage.org/background/law-suit/ProAmicusBriefs.html>, accessed on 2 Apr. 1999.

218 S. Billenness, 'Burma Law on Trial,' *supra* n. 211, p. 1.

219 Ibid., p. 5.

220 Ibid., p. 4

221 Public Citizen/Global Trade Watch, 'Federal Appeals Court Rules Against MA Burma Law' (23 June 1999), <http://www.citizen.org/pctrade/burma/update2.htm>, accessed on 30 July 1999; Judgement in the case of *National Foreign Trade Council* v. *Natsios and Anderson*, United States Court of Appeals for the First Circuit (22 June 1999), <http://www.law.emory.edu/1circuit/june99/98-2304.01a.html>, accessed on 30 July 1999.

222 V. Kroa and S. Billenness, 'Massachusetts to Appeal Burma Law Ruling to U.S. Supreme Court,' *Investing for a Better World* (Sep. 1999), p. 2; E. Iritani, 'Ruling on Myanmar Ban to Go to High Court,' *Los Angeles Times* (13 July 1999), p. C-4, <http://www.latimes.com/>, accessed on 30 July 1999; B. Geman, 'Supreme challenge,' *The Boston Phoenix* (15-22 July 1999), <http://www.bostonphoenix.com/alt1/index.html/archive/features/99/07/15/POLITICS.html>, accessed on 30 July 1999; R. Holding, 'Winds May Be Shifting for S.F.'s Foreign Policy,' *San Francisco Chronicle* (11 July 1999), <http://www.sfgate.com/cgi-bin/article.cgi?file=/chronicle/archive/1999/07/11/SC100286.DTL>, accessed on 30 July 1999.

223 Kroa and Billenness, 'Massachusetts to Appeal Burma Law Ruling to U.S. Supreme Court,' *supra* n. 222, p. 2.

224 L. Miller/Associated Press, 'Burma Law Supporters Stretch from Coast to Coast' (20 Oct. 1999).

225 Ibid.

226 S. Billenness, 'Burma Law on Trial,' *supra* n. 211, p. 5.

227 'Burma government follows ruling on Massachusetts boycott law,' *Boston Globe* (6 Nov. 1998), <http://shweinc.com/news/19981106-3.shtml>, accessed on 15 Apr. 1999.

228 'Advocates vow boycott of companies in Myanmar,' *supra* n. 210.

229 Telephone interview with S. Billenness, Trillium Asset Management, 30 July 1999.

230 'Shell faces Saro-Wiwa legal action,' *Independent on Sunday* (U.K.) (23 May 1999), <http://www.globalarchive.ft.com/search/FTJSPController.htm>, accessed on 30 July 1999; G. Malkani, 'US groups come under spotlight over human rights abroad: An energy company faces the possibility of being held liable for abuses by the Burmese army. Gautam Malkani reports:,' *Financial Times* (5 July 1999), <http://www.globalarchive.ft.com/search/FTJSPController.htm>, accessed on 30 July 1999; E. Press, 'Texaco on Trial,' *The Nation* (31 May 1999), <http://www.thenation.com/>, accessed on 11 Aug. 1999; 'Aguinda v. Texaco; Jota v. Texaco,' <http://www.texacorainforest.org>, accessed on 11 Aug. 1999; Order granting in part and denying in part defendant Unocal's motion to dismiss in case of *Doe* v *Unocal Corp.*, U.S. District Court for the Central District of California (25 Mar. 1997), <http://diana.law.yale.edu/diana/db/31198-1.html>, accessed on 30 July 1999.

231 M. Hood and N. Penniman, 'Environmental, Human Rights and Women's Groups Petition California Attorney General To Revoke UNOCAL's Charter' (10 Sep. 1998), <http://www.igc.org/igc/en/hg/unocal.html>, accessed on 15 Apr. 1999.

232 R. Benson, 'Soft on Crime?' *The Recorder* (San Francisco) (14 Oct. 1998), reproduced as 'Charter Revocation Article Appears in Nationwide Legal Press,' <http://www.heed.net/updates.html> (Update #8, 22 Nov. 1998), accessed on 15 Apr. 1999.

233 Hood and Penniman, 'Environmental, Human Rights and Women's Groups Petition California Attorney General to Revoke UNOCAL's Charter,' *supra* n. 231.

234 'Bar Group Blasts Attorney General's Refusal to Act on Unocal Petition,' <http://www.heed.net/updates.html> (Update #2, 17 Sep. 1998), accessed on 15 Apr. 1999.

235 'Petition Re-filed with Attorney General Lockyer and Governor Davis' (Update #11, 14 Apr. 1999), <http://www.heed.net/update11.html>, accessed on 21 Apr. 1999; 'Action Alert: Attorney General Lockyer turns his back on Unocal petition' (Update #13, 23 June 1999), <http://www.heed.net/update13.html>, accessed on 28 July 1999.

236 'Great News Flash: Huge Victory against Unocal. Oil giant pulls out of Afghanistan due, in part, to our pressure to revoke its charter over women's issue,' <http://www.heed.net/updates.html> (Update #9, 6 Dec. 1998), accessed on 15 Apr. 1999.

237 Benson, 'Soft on Crime?' *supra* n. 232; 'Petition Re-filed with Attorney General Lockyer and Governor Davis,' <http://www.heed.net/update11.html> (Update #11, 14 Apr. 1999), accessed on 21 Apr. 1999.

238 Telephone interview with Professor R. Benson, 22 Apr. 1999; R. Benson, 'Soft on Crime?' *supra* n. 232.

239 J. Wilcox, 'Making the Best of Shareholder Resolutions,' *Insights, the Corporate and Securities Law Advisor*, Vol. 9 (1995), p. 12, referred to in Forcese, *Putting Conscience into Commerce, supra* n. 48, p. 63.

240 S. Billenness, 'Shareholder Activism: Big Oil Takes Some Baby Steps,' in Franklin Research's Insight, *Investing For A Better World* (Sep. 1998), p. 7.

241 *Canadian Press* (16 Jan. 1996), quoted in Forcese, *Putting Conscience into Commerce, supra* n. 48, p. 66.

242 Associated Press/M. Gordon, 'Shareholder Democracy' (1999).

243 See, for example, the following publications by Interfaith Center on Corporate Responsibility: *The Proxy Resolutions Book January 1999* (1999); '1998 Proxy Season Report,' *The Corporate Examiner* Vol. 27, No. 1 (20 Aug. 1998); 'The Shareholder Activism Center,' <http://www.socialfunds.com>, accessed on 22 Apr. 1999.

244 Interfaith Center on Corporate Responsibility, 'Corporate Social Responsibility Challenges 1999,' *The Corporate Examiner*, Vol. 28, No. 3-4 (8 Mar. 1999).

245 Ibid., p. 13.

246 IRRC, *Corporate Social Issues Reporter* (Mar. 1996), p. 2; 'IRRC'

247 IRRC, 'Human Rights and Labor Rights Issues,' IRRC Social Issues Service, 1996 Background Report J.

248 Ibid., 1996 Background Report J:1.

249 Ibid., 1996 Background Report J:2.

250 Ibid., 1996 Background Report J:3.

251 IRRC, *Corporate Social Issues Reporter* (Mar. 1996).

252 Associated Press/M. Gordon, 'Shareholder Democracy' (1999); 'The Shareholder Activism Center,' *supra* n. 243.

253 S. Schueth, 'Social investing,' <http://www.socialfunds.com> (click 'Education,' then 'Social Investing') accessed on 20 Sep. 1999.

254 Ibid.

255 C. Sorrell Jr, 'Socially responsible funds: Human rights and investment,' in Reoch (ed.), *Human Rights: The new consensus, supra* n. 173, pp. 154-55.

256 EIRIS (The Ethical Investment Research Service), 'New funds widen investor choice,' *The Ethical Investor* (Nov./Dec. 1998), p. 2; EIRIS, 'Ethical funds are now worth over £2 billion,' *The Ethical Investor: The EIRIS Guide for Unit Trust Managers* (Mar./Apr. 1999), p. I.

257 Community Growth Fund, *Community Growth Fund and Community Income Fund* (Dec. 1994).

258 Community Growth Fund, *The CGF Report* (30 June 1996); 'Politically correct investment,' supplement to *Mail & Guardian* (South Africa) ('Investing in the Future: Special focus on corporate social responsibility') (27 Mar.-2 Apr. 1998), p. 13.

259 Community Growth Fund, *Community Growth Fund and Community Income Fund* (Dec. 1994).

260 A. Crotty, 'Fund blows the whistle on companies' labour practices,' *Business Report* (South Africa) (15 Dec. 1995).

261 'Investing in upliftment,' supplement to *Mail & Guardian* ('Investing in the Future: Special focus on corporate social responsibility') (27 Mar.-2 Apr. 1998), p. 4; 'A bid to provide real social benefits,' supplement to *Mail & Guardian* ('Investing in the Future: Special focus on corporate social responsibility') (Oct. 1997), p. 18.

262 'www.democracy.com', *The Economist* (3 Apr. 1999), p. 58.

263 'Fighting hypocrisy, injustice and death,' *Upstream: The International Oil & Gas News* (21 Aug. 1998), p. 19.

264 Drucker, *Post-Capitalist Society, supra* n. 1.

265 Figures on market capitalisation from three INTERNET sites on 10 Apr. 1999:

Yahoo!Finance Quotes/Profile <http://quote.yahoo.com/>; Quicken.com Quotes <http://www.quicken.com/investments/snapshot/>; AOL Personal Finance quotes center.

266 *Forbes Global Business & Finance* (17 May 1999), p. 52.

267 A. Abelson, 'Rx for Asia,' Barron's Online (15 Dec. 1997), <http://interactive.wsj.com/pages/barrons.htm>, accessed on 16 Dec. 1997.

268 Drucker, *Post-Capitalist Society, supra* n. 1, p. 182.

269 'With Stock as Bait, Microsoft Lures Elite Professors', *International Herald Tribune* (6 Apr. 1999), p. 1.

270 'The Caux Round Table Principles for Business: An international ethics statement for business' (1994), section 3, <http://www.cauxroundtable.org/ENGLISH.HTM>, accessed on 25 May 1999.

271 The International Code of Ethics for Canadian Business, <http://www.uottawa.ca/hrrec/busethics/codeint.html>, accessed on 28 Mar. 1999.

272 Ibid.

273 J. Schierbeck/Confederation of Danish Industries (Dansk Industri), *Industry and Human Rights* (Apr. 1998).

274 Ibid.

275 Business for Social Responsibility, 'Frequently Asked Questions,' <http://www.bsr.org/>, accessed on 5 June 1999.

276 Business for Social Responsibility, 'Human Rights,' <http://www.bsr.org/resourcecenter/>, accessed on 5 June 1999; Nelson/The Prince of Wales Business Leaders Forum, *Business as Partners in Development, supra* n. 62, p. 267.

277 Business for Social Responsibility, 'Human Rights,' *supra* n. 276.

278 Confederation of Norwegian Business and Industry, 'Checklist for corporations/enterprises interested in investing strategic efforts in human rights issues,' <http://www.nho.no/NHOWEB/nyttogny.nsf/web/english.htm> (click 'Position papers,' then 'Human rights from the perspective of business and industry – a checklist,' then 'Checklist for corporations/enterprises...'), accessed on 14 Sep. 1999.

279 Confederation of Norwegian Business and Industry, 'English version: Human rights from the perspective of business and industry – a checklist,' <http://www.nho.no/NHOWEB/nyttogny.nsf/web/english.htm> (click 'Position papers,' then 'Human rights from the perspective of business and industry – a checklist'), accessed on 14 Sep. 1999.

280 Confederation of Norwegian Business and Industry, 'Business and industry's ethical and social responsibility,' <http://www.nho.no/NHOWEB/nyttogny.nsf/web/english.htm> (click 'Position papers,' then 'Human rights from the perspective of business and industry – a checklist,' then 'Business and industry's ethical and social responsibility'), accessed on 14 Sep. 1999.

281 Ibid.

282 Ibid.

283 M. Williams, 'Private enterprise: Human centred development,' in Reoch (ed.), *Human Rights: The new consensus, supra* n. 173, p. 123.

284 Amnesty International, 'Human Rights Principles For Companies,' *supra* n. 160.

285 ICFTU, 'The ICFTU/ITS Basic Code of Labour Practice,' <http://www.icftu.org/english/tncs/tncscode98.html>, accessed on 28 Mar. 1999.

286 S. Pursey, 'Multinational Enterprises and the World of Work: Globalisation with a Human Face,' <http://www.icftu.org/english/tncs/tncs98ilo.html>, accessed on 28 Mar. 1999.

287 Forcese, *Putting Conscience into Commerce, supra* n. 48, p. 94.

288 ICHRDD, 'Globalisation, Trade and Human Rights,' *supra* n. 68, summary of comments by K. Roth, Executive Director of Human Rights Watch.

289 Levi Strauss & Co, 'Global Sourcing and Operating Guidelines: Evaluation & Compliance,' <http://www.levistrauss.com/about/code.html>, accessed on 27 May 1999.

290 Levi Strauss & Co., 'Global Sourcing and Operating Guidelines: Business Partner Terms of Engagement,' <http://www.levistrauss.com/about/code.html>, accessed on 27 May 1999.

291 Levi Strauss & Co., 'Country Assessment Guidelines,' <http://www.irrc.org/labor/levis.htm>, accessed on 23 May 1999.

292 Ibid.

293 T. Smith, 'Transnational influence: The power of business,' in Reoch (ed.), *Human Rights: The new consensus, supra* n. 173, p. 151.

294 Reebok, 'Reebok Human Rights Production Standards,' *supra* n. 69.

295 Ibid.

296 Reebok, 'About the Reebok Human Rights Award,' <http://www.reebok.com/human-rights/about.html>, accessed on 23 May 1999.

297 The Body Shop, 'Trading Charter,' <http://www.the-body-shop.com/aboutus/body-charter.html>, accessed on 23 May 1999.

298 The Body Shop, *Our Agenda* (1996), p. 6.

299 Ibid., p. 7.

300 The Body Shop, 'Human Rights,' <http://www.the-body-shop.com/aboutus/body-hrights.html>, accessed on 23 May 1999.

301 BP, 'BP's Policy Commitment to Ethical Conduct,' *What we stand for...: Our Business Policies* (Mar. 1998), p. 7; same language in BP Amoco, 'BP Amoco's Policy Commitment to Ethical Conduct,' *What we stand for...Our Business Policies* (Feb. 1999), p. 5.; 'BP Amoco's Policy Commitment to Ethical Conduct,' <http://www.bpamoco.com/about/policies/ethic.htm>, accessed on 23 May 1999.

302 BP, *BP Social Report 1997* (1998), p. 8.

303 Royal Dutch/Shell, 'Statement of General Business Principles,' *supra* n. 32.

304 Royal Dutch/Shell, *Profits and Principles – does there have to be a choice?, supra* n. 101.

305 Ibid., p. 2.

306 Ibid., p. 33.

307 Royal Dutch/Shell, *The Shell Report 1999: People, planet & profits, supra* n. 33, pp. 28-30.

308 Ibid.

309 Ibid., p. 30.

310 'BT calls on Universal Declaration of Human Rights,' *Human rights & Business matters* (Amnesty International UK Business Group Newsletter) (spring 1999), p. 1.

311 Ibid.

312 Government of Canada, *Voluntary Codes: A guide for their development and use* (Mar. 1998), pp. 8-9, quoted in C. Forcese, 'Human Rights Mean Business: Broadening the Canadian Approach to Business and Human Rights,' Feb. 1999 (forthcoming, Proceedings-University of Toronto Human Rights Conference), p. 27.

313 Amnesty International, 'Human Rights Principles For Companies,' *supra* n. 160.

314 Dutch Sections of Amnesty International and Pax Christi International, *Multinational Enterprises and Human Rights, supra* n. 153, p. 59.

315 International Labour Office, Governing Body, Working Party on the Social Dimensions of the Liberalization of Interrnational Trade, 'Overview of global developments and Office activities concerning codes of conduct, social labelling and other private sector initiatives addressing labour issues,' Doc. GB.273/WP/SDL/1 (Rev.1) (Nov. 1998), para. 60, <http://www.ilo.org/public/english/20gb/docs/gb273/sdl-1.htm>, accessed on 19 May 1999.

316 Royal Dutch/Shell, *Business and Human Rights: A Management Primer* (1998), available at <http://www.shell.com/download/3359/index.htm>, accessed on 28 Apr. 1999.

317 Ibid., p. 5.

318 Ibid.

319 Ibid., p. 20.

320 Ibid.

321 Ibid., pp. 20-21.

322 Royal Dutch/Shell, *The Shell Report 1999: People, planet & profits, supra* n. 33, p. 17.

323 BP Amoco, *BP Amoco Environmental and Social Report 1998* (Apr. 1999), p. 38.

324 Statoil, 'People and society,' in *Statoil 1998*, <http://www.statoil.com/STATOILCOM/SVG00990.nsf/eaar/people>, accessed on 9 Apr. 1999.

325 Amnesty International, 'Human Rights Principles For Companies,' *supra* n. 160.

326 The Dutch Sections of Amnesty International and Pax Christi International, *Multinational Enterprises and Human Rights, supra* n.153, p. 59.

327 E. Bernard, 'Ensuring Monitoring is not Coopted,' *New Solutions*, Vol. 7, No. 4 (summer 1997), pp. 10-12; also available at <http://www.tiac.net/users/htup/eb/monitor.html>, accessed on 12 May 1999.

328 Ibid.

329 Ibid.

330 '...Frankental...asks Richard Howitt MEP about the significance of the European Parliament's resolution,' *supra* n. 149, p. 2.

331 U.S. Department of Labor, *The Apparel Industry and Codes of Conduct: A solution to the international child labor problem?* (1996).

332 Browne, 'Corporate Responsibility in an International Context,' *supra* n. 86, p. 9.

333 BP, *BP Social Report 1997* (1998), p. 5.

334 'Sweatshop wars,' *The Economist* (27 Feb. 1999), p. 79.

335 S. Zadek, et al., *Building Corporate Accountability* (London: Earthscan, 1997), pp. 5-6.

336 A. Henriques/New Economics Foundation, 'Are human rights made to measure?' *Human rights and Business matters* (Amnesty International UK Business Group Newsletter) (spring 1999), p. 3.

337 The Tata Iron and Steel Company Limited, *Social Audit Committee: Report* (Bombay: Tata Press Limited, 1980).

338 The Body Shop, 'Founders' Statement,' *The Body Shop Social Statement 95* (1996), p. 3.

339 G. Roddick and A. Roddick, 'Foreword,' in K. Hanson, *Social Evaluation: The Body Shop International – 1995* (1996).

340 K. Hanson, *Social Evaluation: The Body Shop International – 1995* (1996), p.3.

341 *The Times* (London) (19 Sep. 1996).

342 The Body Shop, 'The Body Shop Values Report 1997,' <http:www.the-body-shop.com/aboutus/values.html>, accessed on 27 May 1999.

343 *Resolution Declaration* (22 Mar. 1996); *Statement of Resolution* (15 Dec. 1995); see also P. DeSimone, 'Retailer Bridges the Gap on Supplier Standards,' *IRRC Corporate Social Issues Reporter* (Mar. 1996), pp. 13-16.

344 B. Jeffcott and L. Yanz, 'Exposing the Labour Behind the Label,' *Our Times* (Feb. 1997), <http://www.web.net/~msn/3gap1.htm>, accessed on 17 Apr. 1999.

345 DeSimone, 'Retailer Bridges the Gap on Supplier Standards,' *supra* n. 343, p. 13.

346 'The Gap Agrees to Improve Conditions in Overseas Plants,' *Frontlines* (Jan./Feb. 1996), <http://uaw.org/solidarity/9601/frontlines-jan96.html>, accessed on 17 Apr. 1999.

347 Interfaith Center on Corporate Responsibility, 'STEP TOWARD ELIMINATING SWEAT-SHOPS: The White House Apparel Industry Partnership Report' (undated), <http://www.sweatshopwatch.org/swatch/what/iccr_report.html>, accessed on 28 Mar. 1999.

348 Apparel Industry Partnership, 'Charter Document: Fair Labor Associaton,' Amended Agreement (June 1999), <http://www.lchr.org/sweatshop/amendedFLA.htm>, accessed on 30 July 1999.

349 S. Greenhouse, 'Plan to Curtail Sweatshops Rejected by Union,' *New York Times* (5 Nov. 1998), <http://www.igc.org/swatch/head-lines/1998/aip_nov98.html>, accessed on 13 May 1999.

350 Sweatshop Watch, 'White House Apparel Industry Partnership Issues Proposal with serious shortcomings in living wages and the right to organize,' <http://www.igc.org/swatch/head-lines/1998/aip_nov98.html>, accessed on 13 May 1999.

351 Apparel Industry Partnership, 'Workplace Code of Conduct,' <http://www.lchr.org/sweatshop/amendedFLA.htm#CONDUCT>, accessed on 30 July 1999.

352 'Agreement, What Agreement?: Apparel Industry Partnership,' *Business Ethics*, Vol. 13, No. 1 (Jan./Feb. 1999), p. 8.

353 Apparel Industry Partnership, 'Principles of Monitoring,' <http://www.lchr.org/sweat-shop/amendedFLA.htm#PRINCIPLES>, accessed on 30 July 1999.

354 'UNITE Statement on the White House Apparel Industry Partnership,' <http://www.igc.org/swatch/head-lines/1998/aip_nov98.html>, accessed on 13 May 1999.

355 Greenhouse, 'Plan to Curtail Sweatshops Rejected by Union,' *supra* n. 349.

356 Ibid.

357 'Statement from the Interfaith Center on Corporate Responsibility: Religious Investor Coalition Declines To Endorse Apparel Industry Partnership Agreement,' <http://www.igc.org/swatch/head-lines/1998/aip_nov98.html>, accessed on 13 May 1999.

358 Apparel Industry Partnership, 'Charter Document: Fair Labor Associaton,' Amended Agreement (June 1999), <http://www.lchr.org/sweatshop/amendedFLA.htm>, accessed on 30 July 1999.

359 Greenhouse, 'Plan to Curtail Sweatshops Rejected by Union,' *supra* n. 349.

360 American Council on Education Press Release, 'Fair Labor Association Adds Colleges and Universities, Will Monitor Anti-Sweatshop Labor Standards' (15 Mar. 1999), <http://www.lchr.org/sweatshop/aipalert0399.htm>, accessed on 15 May 1999.

361 Apparel Industry Partnership, 'Organizations Affiliated with the Fair Labor Association as of July 12, 1999,' <http://www.lchr.org/sweat-shop/orgs.htm>, accessed on 17 Aug. 1999; 'PR Newswire: Levi Strauss & Co. joins Fair Labor Association,' 20 July 1999, <http://www.globalarchive.ft.com/search/FTJSPController.htm>, accessed on 5 Aug. 1999; Fair Labor Association, 'Charles Ruff Named First Fair Labor Association Chair, Board of Directors,' (9 Sep. 1999), <http://www.lchr.org/media/fla0999.htm>, accessed on 16 Sep. 1999.

362 Fair Labor Association, 'Charles Ruff Named First Fair Labor Association Chair,' *supra* n. 361.

363 Ibid.

364 Apparel Industry Partnership, 'Organizations Affiliated with the Fair Labor Association (as of July 12, 1999),' *supra* n. 361.

365 A. Bernstein, 'Sweatshop Reform: How to Solve the Standoff,' *Business Week* (3 May 1999), p. 186; World Monitors, 'USAS Worker Centered Monitoring Plan Debuts,' World Monitors Newsletter, 29 Sep. 1999, <http://www.worldmonitors.com>, accessed on 8 Oct. 1999; World Monitors, 'Students

Announce Largest Campaign and Denounce the FLA,' World Monitors Newsletter, 20 Oct. 1999, <http://www.worldmonitors.com>, accessed on 20 Oct. 1999.

366 World Monitors, 'Students Announce Largest Campaign and Denounce the FLA,' *supra* n. 365.

367 World Monitors, 'eCLIPS,' World Monitors Newsletter (22 Sep. 1999), <http://www.world-monitors.com>, accessed on 22 Sep. 1999.

368 S. Greenhouse, 'Nike Reveals Information About Overseas Factories,' *International Herald Tribune* (9-10 Oct. 1999), p. 16; Nike, 'Criticize us more accurately,' <http://www.nikebiz.com/labor/index.shtml>, accessed on 19 Oct. 1999.

369 Greenhouse, 'Nike Reveals Information about Overseas Factories,' *supra* n. 368.

370 Verité, 'Verité: Verification in Trade and Export,' <http://www.verite.org>, accessed on 20 Aug. 1999.

371 World Monitors, 'Collegiate Licensing Company Members Join Forces With Verite' (8 Sep. 1999), <http://www.worldmonitors.com>, accessed on 14 Sep. 1999.

372 S. Greenhouse, '4 Companies Gain Accord in Labor Suit,' *New York Times* (10 Aug. 1999), <http://archives.nytimes.com/archives/>, accessed on 15 Aug. 1999; Sweatshop Watch, 'Retailers Agree to Settlement of Class Action Lawsuit Requiring Independent Monitoring of Factory Conditions' (9 Aug. 1999), <http://www.sweatshopwatch.org/swatch/marianas/settlement.html>, accessed on 19 Oct. 1999; Sweatshop Watch, 'Additional U.S. Retailers Agree to Join Settlement of Class Action Lawsuit Requiring Independent Monitoring of Factory Conditions' (7 Oct. 1999), <http://www.sweatshopwatch.org/swatch/marianas/settlement.html>, accessed on 19 Oct. 1999.

373 Ibid.

374 Sweatshop Watch, 'Additional U.S. Retailers Agree to Join Settlement of Class Action Lawsuit…,' *supra* n. 372.

375 Reebok, 'Reebok Releases In-depth Report on Conditions in Indonesian Factories' (18 Oct. 1999), <http://www.reebok.com/peduli/peduli.cfm>, accessed on 28 Oct. 1999.

376 G. Krupa, 'Reebok Hailed for Releasing Study of Factory Abuses: Reebok Releases Study Detailing Abuses at Factories in Indonesia,' *The Boston Globe* (19 Oct. 1999), p. C1, <http://www.boston.com/globe/>, accessed on 30 Oct. 1999; J. Pereira, 'Reebok Finds Ills

at Indonesian Factories, Will Push for Reform at Contract Facilities,' Wall Street Journal Interactive Edition (18 Oct. 1999), <http://interactive.wsj.com/documents/search.htm >, accessed on 30 Oct. 1999.

377 P. Fireman, 'Steps We Must Take on Third-World Labour,' *The Washington Post* (17 Oct. 1999), p. B7.

378 Reebok, 'Reebok Releases In-depth Report on Conditions in Indonesian Factories,' *supra* n. 375.

379 Ibid.

380 Ibid.

381 A. Bernstein, 'Sweatshops: No More Excuses,' *Business Week* (8 Nov. 1999), p. 110, <http://www.businessweek.com>, accessed on 1 Nov. 1999.

382 Fireman, 'Steps We Must Take on Third-World Labour,' *supra* n. 377.

383 Krupa, 'Reebok Hailed for Releasing Study of Factory Abuses,' *supra* n. 376.

384 Pereira, 'Reebok Finds Ills at Indonesian Factories, Will Push for Reform at Contract Facilities,' *supra* n. 376.

385 T. Kirchofer/Associated Press, 'Reebok-Human Rights' (18 Oct. 1999).

386 Krupa, 'Reebok Hailed for Releasing Study of Factory Abuses,' *supra* n. 376.

387 Bernstein, 'Sweatshops: No More Excuses,' *supra* n. 381, p. 110.

388 Ibid, p. 112.

389 Ibid.

390 Ibid, p. 110.

391 Ibid, p. 112.

392 Ibid, pp. 110-11.

393 Ibid, p. 112.

394 Council on Economic Priorities, 'CEPAA – A General Introduction,' *supra* n. 176; Bernstein, 'Sweatshop Reform: How to Solve the Standoff,' *supra* n. 365, pp. 186, 188; McIntosh, et al., *Corporate Citizenship, supra* n. 21, pp. 246-49, 294-95.

395 EIRIS (The Ethical Investment Research Service), 'Top auditing firms introduce ethical reporting services,' *The Ethical Investor* (Mar./Apr. 1999), p. 1.

396 Ibid.

397 'Sweatshop wars,' *supra* n. 334, p. 79.

398 J. Woodward, 'Safeguarding reputation,' *Human rights & Business matters* (Amnesty International UK Business Group Newsletter) (spring 1999), p. 3.

399 Nike, 'Nike responds to Sweatshop Allegations,' Nike press release (6 June 1996).

400 Global Exchange, 'An Open Letter to Nike Shareholders, Workers, and Consumers from

the Global Exchange Fact-Finding Mission to Indonesia' (16 Sep. 1996).

401 IMGES, *Eliminating Sweatshop Practices* (San Salvador: IMGES, Apr. 1997), quoted in Forcese, *Putting Conscience into Commerce, supra* n. 48, p. 27.

402 International Labour Office, Governing Body, Working Party on the Social Dimensions of the Liberalization of International Trade, 'Overview of global developments and Office activities concerning codes of conduct, social labelling and other private sector initiatives addressing labour issues,' Doc. GB.273/WP/SDL/1 (Rev.1) (Nov. 1998), para. 65, <http://www.ilo.org/public/english/20gb/docs/gb273/sdl-1.htm>, accessed on 19 May 1999.

403 Interfaith Center on Corporate Responsibility, 'A Step Towards Eliminating Sweatshops: The White House Apparel Industry Partnership Report,' <http://www.sweatshopwatch.org/swatch/what/iccr_report.html>, accessed on 28 Mar. 1999.

404 Roddick and Roddick, 'Foreword,' *supra* n. 339.

405 NetAid, 'Why NetAid?' <http://www.netaid.org/netaid/index.htm>, accessed on 14 Sep. 1999.

406 NetAid, 'Our Mission Today,' <http://www.netaid.org/netaid/mission.htm>, accessed on 14 Sep. 1999.

407 T. Lippman, 'An Unlikely Net Alliance; Cisco, U.N. Plan Site to Fight Third World Poverty,' *Washington Post* (12 Aug. 1999), <http://www.corpwatch.org/trac/corner/worldnews/other/429.html>, accessed on 14 Sep. 1999.

408 Ibid.

409 Ibid.

410 NetAid home page, <http://www.netaid.org/index.htm>, accessed on 14 Sep. 1999.

411 Ibid.

412 S. Schiesel, 'With Concerts and Web Site, U.N. Agency Attacks Poverty,' *New York Times* (12 Aug. 1999), <http://www.nytimes.com/library/tech/99/08/biztech/articles/12aid.html>, accessed on 14 Sep. 1999.

413 T. Lippman, 'An Unlikely Net Alliance,' *supra* n. 407.

414 NetAid, 'Clinton, Mandela and Blair Make First Hits on NetAid Website,' <http://www.netaid.org/press/47.htm>, accessed on 14 Sep. 1999.

415 Ibid.

416 Transnational Resource and Action Center (TRAC), 'Key United Nations Agency Solicits Funds from Corporations' (12 Mar. 1999), <http://www.corpwatch.org/trac/undp/undp-press.html>, accessed on 15 Sep. 1999; 'A Letter From International Human Rights, Environment and Development Organizations to James Gustave Speth, Administrator of the UNDP, Maarch 12, 1999,' <http://www.corpwatch.org/trac/undp/letter.html>, accessed on 14 Sep. 1999; 'UNDP Administrator James Gustave Speth's Response, March 17, 1999,' <http://www.corpwatch.org/trac/undp/response.html>, accessed on 14 Sep. 1999; 'The Reply to Mr. Speth from International Human Rights, Environment and Development Organizations, April 14, 1999,' <http://www.corpwatch.org/trac/undp/letter2.html>, accessed on 14 Sep. 1999; N. Klein, 'U.N. pact with business masks real dangers,' *The Toronto Star* (19 Mar. 1999), <http://www.igc.org/trac/undp/star.html>, accessed on 14 Sep. 1999; F. Haq/Inter Press Service, 'Report Faults UNDP Partnership with Corporations,' <http://www.igc.org/trac/undp/ips.html>, accessed on 14 Sep. 1999; J. Oleck, 'Will the UN Sell a Seal of Approval?' *Business Week* (22 Mar. 1999) <http://www.igc.org/trac/undp/buswk.html>, accessed on 14 Sep. 1999; T. Deen/Inter Press Service, 'UN: Pitfalls of Private Sector Involvement' (20 Apr. 1999), <http://www.corpwatch.org/trac/undp/ips2.html>, accessed on 14 Sep. 1999; 'Agency Assailed For Soliciting Money From Companies,' *UN Foundation* (12 Mar. 1999) <http://www.igc.org/trac/undp/unfoundation.html>, accessed on 14 Sep. 1999.

417 TRAC, 'Key United Nations Agency Solicits Funds From Corporations,' *supra* n. 416.

418 Ibid.; TRAC, website concerning UNDP partnership with corporations, <http://www.corpwatch.org/trac/undp/index.html>, accessed on 14 Sep. 1999; Klein, 'U.N. pact with business masks real dangers,' *supra* n. 416.

419 TRAC, 'Key United Nations Agency Solicits Funds From Corporations,' *supra* n. 416; Klein, 'U.N. pact with business masks real dangers,' *supra* n. 416.

420 Ibid.

421 Deen/IPS, 'UN: Pitfalls of Private Sector Involvement,' *supra* n. 416; see also 'UNDP Administrator James Gustave Speth's Response,' *supra* n. 416.

422 Ibid.

423 Deen/IPS, 'UN: Pitfalls of Private Sector Involvement,' *supra* n. 416.

424 U.N. World Food Program, 'The Hunger Site', <http://www.thehungersite.com>, accessed on 20 Sep. 1999.

425 World Bank, 'About BPD: What is Business Partners for Development (BPD)?,' <http://www.worldbank.org/bpd/about.htm>, accessed on 20 May 1999.

426 World Bank, 'About BPD: Why do we need BPD [Business Partners for Development]?,' <http://www.worldbank.org/bpd/about.htm>, accessed on 20 May 1999.

427 World Bank, 'BPD Partners,' <http://www.worldbank.org/bpd/partners.htm>, accessed on 20 May 1999.

428 World Bank, Business Partners for Development, memo (Apr. 1999).

429 Kennedy, 'API: Petroleum execs face non-market pressures,' *supra* n. 83.

430 Daviss, 'Profits from Principle,' *supra* n. 79, p. 33.

431 Chandler, 'The New Corporate Challenge,' *supra* n. 164, p. 68.

432 G. Chandler, 'The wages of oppression,' *Financial Times* (10 Dec. 1998).

433 'Shell to consult pressure groups,' *Financial Times* (17 Mar. 1997).

434 Chandler, 'Oil Companies and Human Rights', *supra* n. 103, p. 5.

435 Schwartz and Gibb, *When Good Companies Do Bad Things*, *supra* n. 28, pp. 177-78.

436 Chandler, 'Oil Companies and Human Rights', *supra* n. 103, p. 5.

437 Chandler, 'Do the Right Thing,' *supra* n. 195, p. 23.

438 Drucker, *Drucker on Asia*, *supra* n. 94, p. 126.

439 Ibid., pp. 126-27.

440 Chandler, 'Do the Right Thing,' *supra* n. 195, pp. 22-23.

441 The Economist Intelligence Unit, 'Just don't,' *Business Asia: Fortnightly Report to Managers of Asia Operations* (28 July 1997), pp. 1-2.

442 Ibid., p. 1.

443 Chandler, 'The New Corporate Challenge,' *supra* n. 164, p. 68.

444 The Economist Intelligence Unit, 'Just don't,' *supra* n. 441, p. 2.

445 Ibid.

446 Chandler, 'Do the Right Thing,' *supra* n. 195, p. 23.

447 D. Lamb, 'Job Opportunity or Exploitation,' *Los Angeles Times* (business section) (18 Apr. 1999); Global Exchange, 'An Open Letter to Nike Shareholders, Workers, and Consumers…,' *supra* n. 400.

448 E. Bernard, 'Ensuring Monitoring is not Coopted,' *supra* n. 327, pp. 10-12.

449 United Press International, 'Indonesian worker outside NikeTown' (22 July 1996).

450 Nike, 'Nike Responds to Sweatshop Allegations,' *supra* n. 399.

451 Ibid.

452 Philip Knight (Nike Chairman and CEO), 'To Our Shareholders' (June 1996).

453 Reuter, 'Rally seeks higher pay for Nike Indonesia workers' (15 July 1996); United Press International, 'Indonesian worker outside NikeTown' (22 July 1996); Associated Press, 'Nike Contests Sweatshop Charge' (17 Sep. 1996); Nike, 'Nike Responds to Sweatshop Allegations,' *supra* n. 399; Philip Knight (Nike Chairman and CEO), 'To Our Shareholders' (June 1996).

454 Global Exchange, 'An Open Letter to Nike Shareholders, Workers, and Consumers…,' *supra* n. 400.

455 'Andrew Youngs Report,' <http://207.87.4.130/social/labor/ay.html>, accessed on 20 Apr. 1999.

456 Ibid.; L. Himelstein, 'Commentary: Nike hasn't scrubbed its image yet,' *Business Week* (7 July 1997), p. 32; Asia Monitor Resource Centre and Hong Kong Christian Industrial Committee, 'Working Conditions in Sports Shoe Factories in China Making Shoes for Nike and Reebok' (Sep. 1997), <http://www.summersault.com/~agj/clr/alerts/hong_kong_reports_3.html>, accessed on 18 Apr. 1999.

457 S. Beck, 'Nike in sweat over heat raised by claims of biased assessment,' *South China Morning Post* (6 July 1997), Money p. 2, <http://www.saigon.com/~nike/news/scmp2.htm>, accessed on 18 Apr. 1999.

458 Asia Monitor Resource Centre and Hong Kong Christian Industrial Committee, 'Working Conditions in Sports Shoe Factories in China…,' *supra* n. 456.

459 Ibid., Himelstein, 'Commentary: Nike hasn't scrubbed its image yet,' *supra* n. 456, p. 32; 'Letter to Andrew Young' (4 Dec. 1997) <http://www.summersault.com/~agj/clr/alerts/letter_to_andrew_young.html>, accessed on 9 June 1999; Letter to the editor of *The Business Journal* (Portland, Oregon, U.S.) from Thuyen Nguyen, Vietnam Labor Watch, 9 July 1997, <http://www.saigon.com/nike/pr5.html>, accessed on 9 June 1999; The Just Don't Do It Campaign at the University of Michigan, 'Nike drops the ball – the Andrew Young Report,' <http://www-personal.umich.edu/~lormand/nike/nike101-5.htm>, accessed on 18 Apr. 1999

460 'Conditions Assailed at Nike Plant,' *International Herald Tribune* (10 Nov. 1997).

461 Complaint in the case of *Mark Kasky* (on behalf of the general public of the State of California) v. *Nike, Inc.* (20 Apr. 1998), <http://www.corpwatch.org/trac/nike/lawsuit.html>, accessed on 26 Apr. 1999.

462 'USA: Nike sued over sweatshop conditions' (20 Apr. 1998), <http://diana.law.yale.edu/diana/db/5798-3.html>, accessed on 19 Apr. 1999.

463 Ibid.

464 Ibid.

465 Complaint in the case of *Mark Kasky, supra* n. 461.

466 Defendants Nike…reply memorandum in support of demurrer to plaintiff's first amended complaint in the case of *Mark Kasky* (on behalf of the general public of the State of California) v. *Nike, Inc.*, San Francisco Superior Court (23 Oct. 1998).

467 'Nike Wins Dismissal of Suit Alleging It Runs Asian Sweatshops,' *International Herald Tribune* (8 Feb. 1999).

468 Ibid.; Telephone interview with law firm of Bushnell, Caplan & Fielding (attorneys for plaintiff), 19 Apr. 1999.

469 Appellant's opening brief, *Kasky* v. *Nike, Inc.*, Case No. A086142 San Francisco Superior Court.

470 E.J. Dionne Jr, 'Swoosh! Public Shaming Nets Results,' *International Herald Tribune* (15 May 1998); 'Critics Force Changes on Nike,' *International Herald Tribune* (14 May 1998).

471 Ibid.

472 Lamb, 'Job Opportunity or Exploitation,' *supra* n. 447.

473 Nike, 'Progress report on key manufacturing initiatives as pledged by Nike CEO Philip H. Knight in May, 1998.'

474 Telephone interview with Vada Manager, Nike (22 Apr. 1999).

475 International Youth Foundation, 'Who We Are,' <http://www.iyfnet.org/who/who.html>, accessed on 18 May 1999.

476 International Youth Foundation, 'Global Alliance formed to enhance workers' lives,' <http://www.iyfnet.org/globalalliance.html>, accessed on 18 May 1999.

477 Ibid.

478 'Global Alliance for Workers and Communities: Program Overview'.

479 Telephone interview with staff at Global Alliance for Workers and Communities, 21 May 1999.

480 Nike, 'Progress report…,' *supra* n. 473.

481 Campaign for Labor Rights, 'Update on Nike/Vietnam Scandal: Background' (26 Jan. 1999), <http://www.summersault.com/~agj/clr/alerts/nikevietupdate.html>, accessed on 18 Apr. 1999.

482 Amnesty International news release, 'Fiftieth anniversary of the Universal Declaration of Human Rights' (AI Index ACT 30/26/98, 10 Dec. 1998), <http://www.amnesty.org/news/1998/A30026 98.htm>, accessed on 21 May 1999.

483 U.N. General Assembly, 'Declaration on the Right and Responsibility of Individuals, Groups and Organs of Society to Promote and Protect Universally Recognized Human Rights and Fundamental Freedoms,' adopted 9 Dec. 1998, U.N. Doc. A/RES/53/144 (1999), <http://www1.umn.edu/humanrts/instree/Res_53_144.html>, accessed on 26 May 1999.

484 T. Bissell, 'Analysis of New Developments,' in Campaign for Labor Rights, 'Update on Nike/Vietnam Scandal,' *supra* n. 481.

485 Campaign for Labor Rights, 'Nike ducks responsibility' (2 Feb. 1999), <http://www.summersault.com/~agj/clr/alerts/nikeducksresponsibility.html>, accessed on 18 Apr. 1999.

486 Ibid.

487 Letter from L. Stewart, Vice President, Law & Corporate Affairs, Nike, to Cu Thi Hau, President, Vietnam Confederation of Labour (24 Feb. 1999).

488 Telephone interview with Vada Manager, Nike (22 Apr. 1999).

489 Bernstein, 'Sweatshops: No More Excuses,' *supra* n. 381, p. 111.

490 'Human rights: Western or universal?' will be available at the same website as this report: 'Business and Human Rights: reports by Christopher Avery···links to other websites,' <http://business-humanrights.org> or alternatively <http://business-humanrights.org/index.html>.

491 Universal Declaration of Human Rights, *supra* n. 9, preamble.

492 Chandler, 'Oil Companies and Human Rights', *supra* n. 103, p. 4.

493 'The Caux Round Table Principles for Business,' *supra* n. 270, section 3 (Stakeholder principles: Communities).

494 'Recommendations to a company doing business in China' and 'Recommendations to a company doing business in Colombia' are available at the same website as this report: 'Business and Human Rights: reports by Christopher Avery···links to other websites,'

<http://business-humanrights.org> or alternatively <http://business-humanrights.org/index.html>.

495 Nelson/The Prince of Wales Business Leaders Forum, *Business as Partners in Development*, supra n. 62; see also J. Nelson/The Prince of Wales Business Leaders Forum, *Building competitiveness and communities: How world class companies are creating shareholder value and societal value* (London: The Prince of Wales Business Leaders Forum, 1998).

496 M. Alperson, *Foundations for a New Democracy* (Randburg, South Africa: Ravan Press, 1995).

497 H. Kleinschmidt, 'Corporate do-gooding 'suspect',' supplement to *Mail & Guardian* ('Investing in the Future: Special focus on corporate social responsibility') (Oct. 1997), pp. 4, 6.

498 'Kagiso Trust,' <http://www.amandla.org/za/host/org/kt.html>, accessed on 1 June 1999.

499 Kleinschmidt, 'Corporate do-gooding 'suspect',' supra n 497, p. 4.

500 Ibid., p. 4, 6.

501 P. Sundar, 'Business, Society and Philanthropy,' in *Footprints of Enterprise: Indian Business Through the Ages*, ed. Federation of Indian Chambers of Commerce and Industry (Delhi: Oxford University Press, 1999), p. 261.

502 'Welcome to ActionAid's website,' <http://www.oneworld.org/actionaid/home.html>, accessed on 4 Nov. 1999.

503 'The Prince of Wales Business Leaders Forum,' <http://www.oneworld.org/pwblf/Who/Index.html>, accessed on 4 Nov. 1999.

504 'About Philippine Business for Social Progress,' <http://www.pbsp.org.ph/about.htm>, accessed on 4 Nov. 1999.

505 'NBI: National Business Initiative,' <http://www.nbi.org.za/>, accessed on 4 Nov. 1999.

506 'Involving Businesses in HRD,' <http://www.escap-hrd.org/resources/features/tbird.htm>, accessed on 4 Nov. 1999.

507 Nelson/The Prince of Wales Business Leaders Forum, *Business as Partners in Development*, supra n. 62, pp. 275-77.

508 The Center for Corporate Community Relations at Boston College, 'The Standards of Excellence in Community Relations: Guiding Principles for Community Relations Practice' (1997).

509 Feeney, *Accountable Aid: Local Participation in Major Projects*, supra n.193, pp. 146-49.

510 Kanter, 'From Spare Change to Real Change,' supra n. 76, p. 126.

511 Philippines Commission on Human Rights, *Barangay Human Rights Action Center Handbook* (undated); Discussion with Carlos Medina, Jr., Executive Director, Ateneo Human Rights Center, Manila, 19 Nov. 1996; A. Velasco, 'Prodem-Misor and partners put up first human rights center in the South,' *Quarterly: Ayala Foundation, Inc.* (Apr.-June 1996), p. 8.

512 Ayala Foundation, 'Message of the President and the Executive Director,' *Annual Report 1995*, p. 6.

513 Hoover's Online, company capsule of Tata Enterprises, <http://www.hoovers.com/>, accessed on 21 Aug. 1999.

514 Drucker, *Post-Capitalist Society*, supra n. 1, p. 62.

515 Thurow, *The Future of Capitalism*, supra n. 3, p. 115.

516 C. Derber, *Corporation Nation* (New York: St. Martin's Press, 1998), p. 44.

517 Harvard Law School Human Rights Program, comment by Aaron Bernstein (workplace editor of *Business Week* magazine), *Business and Human Rights: An Interdisciplinary Discussion Held at Harvard Law School in December 1997* (Cambridge, Massachusetts: Harvard Law School Human Rights Program, 1999), p. 24

518 U.N., 'Address by Mr. Kofi Annan to the Chamber of Commerce of the United States of America, Washington, D.C., 8 June 1999,' <http://www.un.org/partners/business/sgstat1.htm>, accessed on 30 July 1999.

519 U.N., 'The Global Compact,' <http://www.un.org/partners/business/globcomp.htm>, accessed on 30 Oct. 1999.

520 ILO, 'ILO Director-General urges business to become 'part of the solution' to challenge of globalization' (5 Nov. 1999), <http://www.ilo.org/public/english/235press/pr/1999/36.htm>, accessed on 16 Nov. 1999.

521 Thurow, *The Future of Capitalism*, supra n. 3, pp. 308-9.

Amnesty International's mandate

Amnesty International is a worldwide voluntary movement of 1.1 million people that works to prevent some of the gravest violations by governments of people's fundamental human rights. The main focus of its campaigning is to:

- free all prisoners of conscience. These are people detained anywhere for their beliefs, or by reason of their ethnic origin, sex, colour, language, national or social origin, economic status, birth, or other status – who have not used or advocated violence;
- ensure fair and prompt trials for political prisoners;
- abolish the death penalty, torture and other cruel treatment of prisoners;
- end extra-judicial executions and 'disappearances'.

Amnesty International, also opposes abuses by opposition groups: hostage-taking, torture and killings of prisoners and other arbitrary killings.

Amnesty International is impartial. It is independent of any government, political persuasion or religious creed. It does not support or oppose any government or political system, nor does it support or oppose views of the victims whose rights it seeks to protect. It is concerned solely with the protection of the human rights involved in each case, regardless of the ideology of the government, opposition forces or the beliefs of the individual. Amnesty International is financed by subscriptions and donations from its world-wide membership. No funds are sought or accepted from governments.

Amnesty International, recognising that human rights are indivisible and inter-dependent, works to promote all the human rights enshrined in the Universal Declaration of Human Rights and other international standards, through its human rights education programmes and campaigning for ratification of human rights treaties.

Index